engage

Welcome to **engage** issue 7. Prepare to be blown away by God's awesome word. Whether you've been a Christian for years, not long at all or you're not even sure you're a Christian, God has loads to say to you. Check out what we've got in store for you in this engage.

[*] **DAILY READINGS** Each day's page throws you into the Bible, to get you handling, questioning and exploring God's message to you — encouraging you to act on it and talk to God more in prayer.

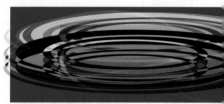

THIS ISSUE: Big plans for God's people in **Ephesians**; Big warnings for Moses and the Israelites in **Numbers;** Big life lessons from Jesus in **Luke;** Big disaster and a big future in **Jeremiah;** and big emotions in **Psalms.**

[*] **TAKE IT FURTHER** If you're hungry for more at the end of an **engage** page, turn to the **Take it further** section to dig deeper.

[*] **TRICKY** tackles those mind-bendingly tricky questions that confuse us all, as well as questions that our friends bombard us with. This time: **Why does God allow suffering?**

[*] **STUFF** Articles on stuff relevant to the lives of young Christians. This issue: **Coping with stress.**

[*] **ESSENTIAL** Articles on the basics we really need to know about God, the Bible and Christianity. This issue, we ask: **What does it mean to be human?**

[*] **REAL LIVES** True stories, revealing God at work in people's lives. This time — **from pauper to prisoner to best-selling author.**

[*] **TOOLBOX** is full of tools to help you wrestle with the Bible. This issue we look at different **genres** in the Bible.

All of us who work on engage are passionate to see God's word at work in people's lives. Do you want God's word to have an impact on your life? Then open your Bible, and start on the first engage study right now...

HOW TO USE engage

1 Set a time you can read the Bible every day

2 Find a place where you can be quiet and think

3 Grab your Bible, pen and a notebook

4 Ask God to help you understand what you read

5 Read the day's verses with engage, taking time to think about it

6 Pray about what you've read

BIBLE STUFF We use the NIV Bible version, so you might find it's the best one to use with engage. If the notes say **'Read Luke 6 v 1–5'**, look up Luke in the contents page at the front of your Bible. It'll tell you which page Luke starts on. Find chapter 6 of Luke, and then verse 1 of chapter 6 (the verse numbers are the tiny ones). Then start reading. Simple.

In this issue...

DAILY READINGS

Ephesians: Big big stuff
Numbers: Counting on God
Luke: Walking with Jesus
Jeremiah: Prophet in pain
Psalms: Down in the depths

ARTICLES

ESSENTIAL
Being human 12

STUFF
Coping with stress 24

TRICKY
Why does God allow suffering? 46

TOOLBOX
Genres in the Bible 60

REAL LIVES
Prisoner's progress 78

TEAM ENGAGE

Star writers: Martin Cole   Cassie Martin   Carl Laferton   Helen Thorne
Head coach: Martin Cole
Kit designer: Steve Devane
Cheerleading proof-readers: Anne Woodcock   Nicole Carter

Ephesians

Big big stuff

How's your relationship with God? Are you zooming along or do you feel like you're stuck in a rut, going nowhere? Whichever is true, Ephesians is the book for you. It's a letter Paul wrote around 60AD to a church in Ephesus (in what is now Turkey).

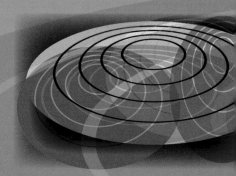

Here are three reasons why Ephesians could change your life:

1. THE BIG PICTURE

Paul opens our eyes to the great plan of God, which started before time began and will continue forever. Paul will reveal to us God's big purposes and show us where Christians fit into His perfect plan. Get ready to have your horizons expanded.

2. BIG TRUTH

Ephesians will help you get your head round what makes Jesus' death on the cross so important. It will show you Jesus' role in God's plan. It will show you what the Holy Spirit does.

And it will reveal to you God's plans for His people.

3. BIG WAY OF LIFE

Paul gives us practical advice on how to live for God in our down-to-earth daily lives. He helps us out of the rut and pushes us forward on God's tracks.

Ephesians divides neatly into two halves. Chapters 1–3 reveal God's plans to create a new people. Chapters 4–6 talk about how God's people should now live. This book is full of life-changing stuff. So what are you waiting for?

Simply the blessed

Ever opened a cupboard so full of stuff that it piles out and falls on your head? Well, the first chapter of Ephesians is like that — it's stuffed full of truths about God that are almost too much to take in.

👁 Read Ephesians 1 v 1–2

ENGAGE YOUR BRAIN

▶ *How does Paul describe himself?*

▶ *And what two phrases describe the Christians in Ephesus? (v1)*

Did you notice the words *grace* and *peace* in v2? Well, keep your eyes open, as both appear loads of times in this letter as major themes. Paul calls himself an apostle of Jesus — someone sent out by God to tell people about Jesus. He describes the Ephesian Christians as 'saints'. That doesn't mean they all have their own special day and bring people luck. *"Saints"* means "holy ones, set aside to serve God". All Christians are saints!

👁 Read verses 3–6

▶ *Why is God worth shouting about? (v3)*

▶ *What has God done exactly? (v4–6)*

Paul doesn't hold back — he hits us with the big stuff right away. God has given us great blessings (privileges). In fact, Paul says we've got all of them (v3). Not one is held back from us. For a glimpse of all that God has done for us, read through verses 4–14. It's mind-blowing.

These blessings are for God's people, Christians. We've not earned them; they're a free gift (v6). Before the universe began, God chose us to be His people (v4). In fact, Christians can call themselves God's sons and daughters (v5). What a privilege.

PRAY ABOUT IT

All of this was made possible by Jesus. Spend time now reading through v1–6 and praising God for all He has done for His people.

THE BOTTOM LINE

God blesses His people. Loads.

➡ TAKE IT FURTHER

More blessings on page 108.

2 | Perfect plan

Paul is so excited about all that God has done, is doing and will do for His people. He's so fired up that (in the original Greek) v3–14 are one long, 200-word sentence! Join in with the excitement.

👁 Read Ephesians 1 v 7–10

ENGAGE YOUR BRAIN
▷ *What has Jesus' death achieved? (v7)*

▷ *What is God's big plan? (v10)*

Christians have so much to thank God for. He redeemed them — bought them back from slavery to sin. It cost the life of His Son. And look what it gave us — true forgiveness. And God even let us in on His perfect plan that will end in Jesus ruling over a new heaven and a new earth. One day, the whole universe will worship Jesus as King.

👁 Read verses 11–14
▷ *What are the steps to becoming one of God's people? (v13)*

▷ *Try putting v13–14 into your own words.*

God chose His people from the beginning of time (v11). But it still requires us to believe that Jesus' death can save us — we must put our trust in Him (v13). Those who do are marked as belonging to God (v13). They receive His Holy Spirit, who guarantees that one day they'll receive everything God has in store for them in His new world. All of this should lead to us praising God big time (v12, v14).

GET ON WITH IT
▷ *How should Ephesians 1 v 1–14 shape your priorities in life?*

▷ *What do you need to change?*

PRAY ABOUT IT
▷ *Which verses make you want to praise God?*
Go on then...

→ TAKE IT FURTHER
Further plans can be found on page 108.

3 Power-filled prayer

We've been reading about the blessings God heaps on believers. Have you grasped how great they are yet? Do you even feel like you're one of God's people? If so, do you feel privileged?

Read Ephesians 1 v 15–19

ENGAGE YOUR BRAIN

▷ *What does Paul pray for these Christians? (v17)*

▷ *What does Paul pray they'll know and understand? (v18–19)*

Paul was so excited to hear these guys in Ephesus had become Christians that he prayed for them all the time — that they would know God better. As Christians grow, they learn and understand more about God. They know that they'll spend eternity with Him and they can know and experience God's power working in their lives. Paul continues...

Read verses 19–23

▷ *Where is Jesus now? (v20)*

▷ *How would you describe Jesus' greatness? (v20–23)*

When Jesus died on the cross, God didn't just raise Him back to life;

He raised Him to a new life as ruler over everyone and everything. He is head of the church — that means all Christians. If you're a believer, Jesus is your boss.

PRAY ABOUT IT

Paul prays that God's people will know God's power in their lives — the power which raised Jesus from death to be head of the universe and head of God's people. Just think how that power can help us live for Him.

▷ *Read verses 15–19 and pray those same things for Christians you know, and for yourself.*

THE BOTTOM LINE
Jesus rules.

→ TAKE IT FURTHER
More prayer pointers on page 108.

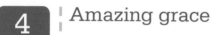

4 Amazing grace

What makes someone a Christian?
Can we do anything to get right with God?

Read Ephesians 2 v 1–7

ENGAGE YOUR BRAIN

▷ How does Paul describe life before being rescued by Jesus? (v1–3)

▷ What has God done? (v5–6)

▷ Why? (v4, v7)

Before you trust in Jesus, you're **dead**, a slave to sin and heading towards punishment from God. It's horrible. But because God loves us so ridiculously much, He sent His Son to rescue us and give us new life. Just in case you think you deserve it, listen carefully to Paul...

Read verses 8–10

▷ How much are we responsible for this new life?

▷ So how should Christians now live? (v10)

Our new life, freedom and rescue are all down to God. We're full of sin, so we don't deserve God's love and rescue. Yet He gives it to us anyway. That's what **grace** is — God sending His Son to die for us despite us deserving His punishment. When we turn to Jesus, God makes us into something new, so that we can serve Him in great ways. It's all part of His perfect plan (v10).

GET ON WITH IT

Think about what God has done for you through Jesus and what He has promised to do for you in the future.

▷ How should this knowledge change your priorities and the way you live?

PRAY ABOUT IT

Read today's verses again and then talk honestly with God, straight from your heart.

→ TAKE IT FURTHER

Find yourself on page 108.

5 | Free peace, sweet!

Jews = God's chosen people. Gentiles = everyone else. God intended the Jews to bring Gentiles to know Him. But instead they hated Gentiles, who in turn hated them. But God had other plans for them both...

👁 Read Ephesians 2 v 11–13

ENGAGE YOUR BRAIN

▷ *What used to be true for Gentiles? (v12)*

▷ *What changed all that? (v13)*

👁 Read verses 14–18

▷ *What has Jesus done for Jews and Gentiles? (v14)*

▷ *So what's true for all believers, whether Jew or Gentile? (v18)*

Jesus broke down the barrier that kept Gentiles far from God and at war with Jews. Jesus' purpose was to create *"one new man"* (v15) — a new human race, made up of Jews and Gentiles united with each other and friends with God. That's the church — God's people of all backgrounds who have access to God (v18).

👁 Read verses 19–22

▷ *Who's at the centre of God's people? (v20–21)*

▷ *What's the great news for Christians? (v22)*

All believers are united through Christ, and are part of God's family. Jesus is at the centre of this family. Mind-blowing fact: God lives in the lives of His people, through the Holy Spirit!

GET ON WITH IT

▷ *How can you get on better with believers you know who are different from you?*

▷ *If God's Spirit lives in you, how can you be a better home for Him?*

THE BOTTOM LINE

Jesus brings us nearer to God and to each other.

→ TAKE IT FURTHER

Break down barriers on page 109.

6 Open secret

What's the best secret you've ever kept? What happened when you revealed it? Paul now tells us about a big secret, or "mystery". Except it hadn't been kept very secret at all...

👁 Read Ephesians 3 v 1–6

ENGAGE YOUR BRAIN

▷ *What's the mystery that has now been revealed? (v6)*

It's not a secret any more — anyone can be part of God's family and share in God's great promises. Just like Paul, we're privileged to be let in on this secret. We should thank God for these great truths.

👁 Read verses 7–13

▷ *What was Paul's job description? (v7–9)*

▷ *What great result of Jesus' work must we remember? (v12)*

Paul was to preach the good news of Jesus to Gentiles (non-Jews) and tell everyone the role of God's people. The whole process would teach unseen spiritual beings God's great plan (v10). Incredible stuff!

PRAY ABOUT IT

Just as amazing is the fact that we can *"approach God with freedom and confidence"*. How awesome is that? So what are you waiting for? Approach God freely and confidently right now, telling Him what's on your mind.

THE BOTTOM LINE

Anyone can share in God's promises and get to know Him personally.

→ TAKE IT FURTHER

No secrets on page 109.

7 | Paul's powerful prayer

Today Paul tells us some big truths about God and gives us some top tips on praying for other Christians.

👁 **Read Ephesians 3 v 14–21**

ENGAGE YOUR BRAIN

You're doing all the work today — figuring out what Paul is teaching us.

▷ First, write down what we learn about God.
▷ v16:

▷ v18:

▷ v20:

God's love is so deep, wide, long and high that it's too much for us to fully understand. Yet we can talk to this incredible God. And here's how...

👁 **Read verses 14–21 again**

▷ Put into your own words what Paul prays for these Christians.
▷ Strength (v16–17):

▷ Love for each other (v17):

▷ Knowledge (v18–19):

PRAY ABOUT IT

Look back on the notes you made. Spend 5 minutes thanking and praising God for the first set of things you wrote down. Then spend a further 5 minutes, using the other stuff you wrote down, to pray for Christians you know.

→ **TAKE IT FURTHER**

Keep praying on page 109.

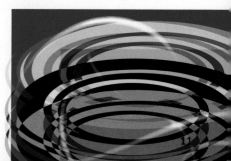

8 One faith, one Lord

We've read loads about what God has done for us. But what should we do to serve Him? And for other believers? How do we actually live as Christ-followers?

Read Ephesians 4 v 1–2

ENGAGE YOUR BRAIN

▷ *What does Paul want us to do? (v1)*

▷ *What five qualities should Christians show? (v2)*

GET ON WITH IT

Next to each quality, write the name of a Christian you know and how you can show that characteristic to them.

Humble:

Gentle:

Patient:

Bearing with them:

Love:

Read verses 3–6

▷ *How seriously should Christians take the issue of unity? (v3)*

▷ *How might the qualities in v2 achieve unity among Christians?*

God's people should show unity because God is in perfect unity — Father, Son and Spirit. It won't just happen instantly, but we must keep working on showing humility, gentleness, patience and love to each other.

PRAY ABOUT IT

Which one of the qualities from v2 do you need most help with? Talk to God and ask for His help.

THE BOTTOM LINE

Christians must work at being united.

→ TAKE IT FURTHER

United we stand... on page 109.

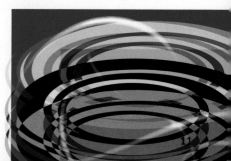

ESSENTIAL

Being human

In *Essential*, we take time out to explore key truths about God, the Bible and Christianity. This issue, we're looking in the mirror at ourselves. What does it mean to be human?

Who am I? What's the point of me? How does God feel about me? Are humans merely mammals? Genetic accidents? Products of our upbringing? Are we whatever we choose to be? If you've ever asked a question like that, then here are six fantastic facts, straight from the Bible, to help you get your head round the wonderful world of you.

PRECIOUS

We are no accident. No random product of nature. We are loved and we're here for an important purpose. God made each of us — He was at work choosing the colour of our eyes and deciding how big our nose was going to be long be before we were born (Psalm 139 v 13). He knows the number of hairs on our head (Luke 12 v 7). And provides for our needs (Luke 12 v 22–31). He has made us to be little visual aids of what He is

like (that's what it means to be made in God's image) and has designed us so we can give and receive love from Him and from other people. On top of all that He's given us the job of helping to look after His planet (Genesis 1 v 27–28). All this means we are precious beyond measure, loved more than words can express and our lives are packed full of purpose. Amazing.

REBELLIOUS

But we are far from perfect! If you've ever felt as though you mess up all the time and continually let down God and other people... welcome to the human race! None of us naturally does what God wants (Romans 3 v 23). All of us get things wrong (Psalm 14 v 2–3). We live life our way instead of God's way and in doing so, we all walk away from God — that's what the Bible calls **sin**.

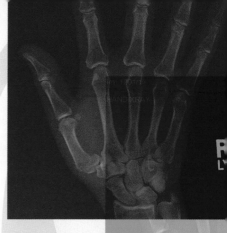

WANTED

Being a mess doesn't stop God from wanting us in His family. We may have wandered away from Him but He wants us back! He is a good Father who is willing to offer unconditional love to any of His children who come home (Luke 15 v 11–31). In fact, He is the best kind of Father — one who will actively come looking for us, even when we have rejected Him (Luke 15 v 1–7).

For those of us who are Christians, there are three other things that are true of us. We are:

FORGIVEN

Jesus' death and resurrection was awesome. He took the punishment that we deserve. And He made it possible for us to be made clean. Every lie, angry word, unkind action and sinful thought has been dealt with. Not one remains. Nothing is too bad or too serious or too hard for Jesus to sort out. We are forgiven. Free. And brought back into God's family (Romans 5 v 6–11).

GIFTED

There is no such thing as a useless Christian. Every single one of us has gifts from God to use in serving Him. God helps some of us teach and lead. Others He blesses with money so we can give generously. Others are good at encouraging the people around us. The list of gifts is long and varied! And every person has a gift that is needed to make the church work well — that's one of the reasons why it's so important we're part of a church family (Romans 12 v 3–8).

CHANGING

Every day the Holy Spirit is at work in us, changing us to be more like Jesus. Like a tree bearing fruit, we gradually show more and more of God's love and priorities. We are becoming more loving, more patient, more kind and more self-controlled (Galatians 5 v 22–23). We may have a way to go — but the change is happening. We are becoming the people that God wants us to be. And one day we can look forward to eternity where we will be perfect (yes, really!) and will enjoy a perfect relationship with God for ever (Revelation 21 v 1–4).

That's us. That's you! If you want to find out more, why not get hold of a copy of: *Mirror, Mirror* by Graham Beynon, available on the Good Book Company website.

Numbers

Counting on God

Numbers. Not the most exciting name for a book, is it? You might as well call it "Calculations" or "Moses and Maths".

Expect loads of numbers in this book. It begins and ends with a couple of population counts — in the 40 years in between, the number of Israelites stays almost exactly the same. That's disappointing when you think back to God's promise to Abraham that one day his descendants would be impossible to count.

But looking at it from another angle, once we get into the heart of the book, it's amazing that there are any Israelites left at all after those 40 years — it's just one long catalogue of grumbling and rebellion followed by God's terrifying judgment.

Why is this relevant for Christians today? **Read 1 Corinthians 10 v 1–11 to find out.**

All of the things that happened to the Israelites in the wilderness are recorded as warnings for us. Yep, that includes you!

And just as you'd be pretty silly to ignore a warning like this,

you'd be equally dumb to ignore the warnings we find in the book of Numbers!

Numbers? Check. Warnings? Check. But most importantly the book begins and ends with God's plans for His people. Plans to bring them into a wonderful land, to prosper them and to be with them. You can count on God.

9 ¦ Count me in

The story so far: the Israelites have been rescued from slavery in Egypt, and are heading for rest in the promised land, but not there yet. We can learn loads about what to expect by looking at their preparations.

There's loads to read in this first section, but whizz through it to get the big picture of what was going on.

👁 Read Numbers 1 v 1–19

ENGAGE YOUR BRAIN

▷ Who were Moses and Aaron to count? (v3)

▷ How many times are we reminded of this? (Skim the rest of the chapter, v20, v22, v24 etc)

▷ What does this tell us about what the Israelites were to expect on this next part of their journey?

👁 Skim read chapters 2–4

▷ What (or who) is at the heart of the Israelite camp? (2 v 1)

▷ The preparations aren't just for battle — what else? (4 v 46–49)

▷ How is this encouraging, given what we know they were to expect on their journey?

Exciting that God was with the Israelites, but also dangerous — like travelling with dynamite. The specially purified Levites acted as a kind of buffer zone around the tabernacle.

There is a lot of detail and a lot of counting going on in these early chapters of Numbers. But all the preparations must be made before the people can set out on the next phase of their journey.

PRAY ABOUT IT

Thank God that Christians are even better off than the Israelites. Whatever we face in life, God is with us by His Spirit (Matthew 28 v 20).

THE BOTTOM LINE

God is with us in life's battles.

→ TAKE IT FURTHER

Time for a rest on page 109.

10 Gifts to God

The preparations are still going on, as God's people get ready to hit the promised land. They aren't just getting ready for a fight though; they need to be holy too.

👁 Speed read chapters 5 and 6

These chapters seem quite bizarre and maybe a little harsh too, but God is really concerned about faithfulness in all relationships. He is pure and holy and totally trustworthy and He wants His people to be the same.

ENGAGE YOUR BRAIN

▷ *Heavy responsibilities, yes, but what blessings did the Israelites receive? (end of 5 v 3 and 6 v 22–27)*

▷ *How are Christians blessed like this today?*

👁 Skim read chapters 7 and 8

▷ *Chapters 7 and 8 list all the gifts that the Israelites offered to God — but what do you notice about the Levites? (8 v 13)*

The Levites themselves were gifts to God. Similarly Christians offer themselves to God as a response to His great kindness and mercy in rescuing them.

They give their lives to serving Him.

GET ON WITH IT

Read Romans 12 v 1–2 and think about how you can offer yourself to God as a "living sacrifice" — look especially at v2 for ideas and think about what that will mean for you this week.

THE BOTTOM LINE

God blesses His people and they in turn live for Him.

→ TAKE IT FURTHER

Time for a singalong on page 109.

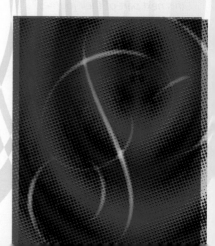

11 | Moving on

We've had hints of this already, but now God reminds the Israelites in a big way that He is with them and will guide them on their journey, just as He had been doing since the first Passover in Egypt.

👁 Read Numbers 9 v 1–23

ENGAGE YOUR BRAIN

▷ Look at v1–5. Can you remember what event the Passover commemorated? (Exodus chapter 12)

▷ Why was it so important that Israel remembered this event?

▷ Read v17–18. How many times is this repeated in the rest of chapter 9? Get the point?

The cloud symbolised God's presence with His people and showed He was guiding them every step of the way.

PRAY ABOUT IT

Ask God to help you remember Him rescuing you through Jesus' death. Thank Him for being with you every day of your life.

👁 Read Numbers 10 v 1–36

Eleven months after arriving at Sinai, God's people broke camp and moved on — the first steps towards the promised land. They marched on obediently in organised formation (v14–28). They took the tabernacle with them too. So far so good.

▷ What's so great about v29?

▷ What's wonderful about v35–36?

It's looking so good, but within three days it all goes horribly wrong... Despite God travelling with His sinful people, they remained precisely that: a sinful people.

PRAY ABOUT IT

One of Jesus' titles is *Emmanuel* which means *God is with us*. Thank God that He sent Jesus to deal with human sin once and for all.

THE BOTTOM LINE

God is with His people.

→ TAKE IT FURTHER

Move along to page 110.

12 | Moaning Miriam

And it was all looking so good. But the whining starts again as the Israelites hit the road. Three grumbling complaints from the Israelites and three responses from God: punishment, mercy, and then a bit of both.

◉ Read Numbers 11 v 1–35

ENGAGE YOUR BRAIN

▷ What are they grumbling about?
11 v 1:
11 v 4–6:
12 v 1–2:
▷ Why are v4–6 so outrageous?
▷ Who are they really grumbling about?

Moses also seems to be moaning (v10–15) but there's a big difference — he complains *to* God, not *about* God. One is a sign of unbelief, the other a sign of faith.

PRAY ABOUT IT

Is there anything you need to honestly talk to God about now? Take your problems to Him; don't just whine about them to other people.

▷ How does God encourage Moses? (v17)
▷ What does He remind Moses of? (v23)

▷ How does He answer his people? (v18–20)

◉ Read Numbers 12 v 1–16

▷ What is Miriam's problem? (v1-2)
▷ What's the real issue?
▷ What is God's reaction?
▷ How does Miriam's sin affect everyone? (v15)

It seems a bit harsh that Miriam gets zapped and Aaron doesn't, but notice that she's the ringleader. Her name appears first and the Hebrew language in these verses is feminine, suggesting she is doing the speaking! God is always just and fair.

PRAY ABOUT IT

Do you compare yourself to others? *"Why does he/she always get chosen to do things in the youth service? I'm just as good!"* Notice what Numbers 12 v 3 says about Moses. Do you need to pray for that attitude?

→ TAKE IT FURTHER

Moanathon on page 110.

13 | Your number's up

So near and yet so far... you can almost taste the milk and honey. Just as the Israelites reach the edge of the promised land, it all goes horribly wrong.

👁 **Speed read chapter 13**

ENGAGE YOUR BRAIN

▶ *What promise does God remind His people of in v2?*

Verses 17-25 echo God's words to Abraham when God first promised him this land (Genesis 13 v 14–17). God's promises may take a while but He always keeps His word.

▶ *What is the promised land like? (v23, v27)*

▶ *What are most of the spies afraid of? (v28)*

▶ *How do they exaggerate? (v32)*

Only Joshua and Caleb show faith in God's promises (13 v 30 and 14 v 6–9), despite God showing Israel time and time again that He can and will do what He has promised.

👁 **Skim read chapter 14**

▶ *Why are v4 and 10 so awful?*

▶ *How does God see their behaviour? (v11–12)*

▶ *What reasons does Moses give for why God should spare His people? (v13–19)*

▶ *What is God's final verdict? (v28–35)*

Too late, the people realise how sinful they have been and try to take matters into their own hands (v39–45). But without God they can do nothing — a lesson it will take them 40 years in the desert to learn.

PRAY ABOUT IT
Ask God to help you fear Him and not fear men.

THE BOTTOM LINE
We can trust God's promises.

→ **TAKE IT FURTHER**
More stuff on page 110.

14 | Promises, offerings and tassels

A bit of a shift in tone now as God gives Moses some more laws about how His people are to live. Hardly what you would expect after the drama of the last chapter. Or is it?

👁 Read Numbers 15 v 1–41

ENGAGE YOUR BRAIN

▷ What are all these laws about?
v1-21 :
v22-29:
v30-36:
v37-41:

▷ What had God done for them in the past? (v41)

▷ What did He promise to do in the future? (v2, v18)

▷ Why would this have been encouraging for the whole community after the events of chapter 14?

▷ Why did they do the tassel thing? (v39–40)

GET ON WITH IT

Whether or not you're into tassels, it's a good idea to think of ways to help you remember the way God wants you to live (v39–40). Some people wear *"What Would Jesus Do?"* bracelets, others always pray while they brush their teeth.

▷ What can you do today to help you remember that you belong to God?

PRAY ABOUT IT

Sometimes we sin unintentionally, sometimes deliberately. Thank God for the free forgiveness He offers us through Jesus. Spend some time right now asking for His forgiveness for specific things and thanking Him for His mercy and forgiveness.

THE BOTTOM LINE

God has rescued you. Keep reminding yourself to live for Him.

→ TAKE IT FURTHER

No tassels on page 110.
That's a promise.

15 Carry on grumbling

Another day, another rebellion. God's people still weren't getting the message. Are we any different?

👁 Read Numbers 16 v 1–40

ENGAGE YOUR BRAIN

▶ Who is complaining this time? (v1–2)

▶ What are their two complaints? (v3 and v12–14)

▶ Where have we heard this kind of thing before?

▶ How does God deal with Dathan and Abiram (ordinary Israelites) and the Korahites (Levites who did tabernacle duties) in v25–35?

These grumblers had forgotten one crucial thing — God is utterly holy. By thinking just anyone could rock up to offer Him incense, and ignoring the safeguards God had put in place to enable a sinful people to live near a holy God, they lost their lives.

👁 Read verses 41–50

Scarily verses 41–43 show that the lesson still hadn't been learned.

▶ What danger do the Israelites face?

▶ Who is the only one who can stop God's anger? (v46–48)

Only God's high priest can make atonement for sin — can bring a sinful people safely near to a perfect and holy God. God provided the priest — in this case Aaron — and would one day provide a perfect High Priest to make permanent atonement, between God and man. Jesus Christ.

PRAY ABOUT IT

Thank God for Jesus and His work in making us acceptable to God.

THE BOTTOM LINE

Only Jesus can bring us near to God.

→ TAKE IT FURTHER

Carry on to page 110.

16 Budding career

**More on God's chosen high priest in chapter 17
as God makes it very clear who He has chosen.
And it happens in a really strange way...**

👁 Read Numbers 17 v 1–13

ENGAGE YOUR BRAIN

▶ *What is God wanting to accomplish here? (v5)*

▶ *How does He do it? (v2–7)*

▶ *What makes this sign so dramatic and such decisive proof that Aaron is God's chosen priest? (v8)*

▶ *How do the rest of the Israelites react?*

"Help! Help! We're all going to die!" (v12) Seems like a bit of an over-reaction, given v10. But the people are starting to see that God is not safe. He is holy and perfect. They are disgustingly sinful and dirty compared to God. No wonder they are terrified of Him.

PRAY ABOUT IT

Do you take God for granted? Assume your sin is no big deal? Treat Him like an indulgent grandfather

who will always forgive you? Surely He doesn't care much about your little life and your little sins. Wrong.

Take some time out to think about God's perfection and holiness now and say sorry for treating Him without respect.

THE BOTTOM LINE

God is not safe, He is holy.

→ TAKE IT FURTHER

A little bit more on page 111.

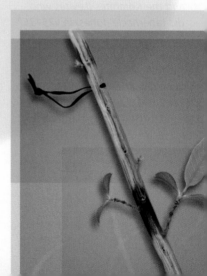

17 | Give it back

How's your memory? Can you remember everyone's birthday, phone number and the names of their pets? Or do you have trouble remembering your own birthday? God now hits the Israelites with some rule reminders.

👁 Read Numbers 18 v 1 –20

ENGAGE YOUR BRAIN

▶ What special responsibilities do the high priest and his family have? (v1, v3–7)

▶ Are there any benefits for Aaron and his family? (v8–19)

▶ What don't they have and why? (v20)

Perhaps it would have been hard missing out when the rest of the Israelites started getting their portions of the land. But how amazing to be told by God that He is your share and inheritance.

👁 Read verses 21–32

▶ What are the Levites to receive in place of their inheritance? (v21)

▶ What must they do with it? (v26)

▶ What would this remind them of?

The tithe was an offering from the people to God. When the Levites received it, they in turn gave some of it back to God. As Psalm 24 v 1 reminds us: *"The earth is the LORD's, and everything in it, the world, and all who live in it"*. Everything is God's so we shouldn't hold stuff back from Him.

GET ON WITH IT

Do you treat your possessions that way? The money you have or earn? Your time and energy? Your skills and abilities? How can you live remembering Psalm 24 v 1 today?

THE BOTTOM LINE

What good is it to gain the whole world yet lose your soul? God is all we need.

→ TAKE IT FURTHER

Chapter 19 isn't missing; it's on page 111.

STUFF

Coping with stress

"I've got too much to do and too little time to do it and I'm not sure I'm up to it and it's all weighing heavily on my mind and... AAAAAARRRGGHHHHH!!!" We can let stress overwhelm us. But we don't have to! The Bible gives us a godly, eternal perspective on our lives and our worries.

PICK YOUR PRIORITIES

It's worth asking yourself if your priorities are the same as God's. Maybe you're worried about getting good qualifications to ensure you do well in life and get a good job and earn enough money. But the Bible says that God is our Provider, and ultimately we need to recognise that we are dependent on Him, not on ourselves.

"Seek first his kingdom and his righteousness, and all these things will be given to you as well" (Matthew 6 v 33).

Getting our priorities straight means putting God first; realising that our exams and our achievements are not the be all and end all. The gospel comes first. Always. Serving God, making sure we give Him our time,

telling others about Jesus — these things must get top priority. Let's face it, our worries and stresses really aren't as important!

GREAT EXPECTATIONS

Some of the stress in our lives can come from a desire to please other people; to live up to the expectations of our parents, teachers or friends. Doing things that matter to them. Achieving so they'll be impressed. It can all put extra pressure on our shoulders.

The simple truth is this: **other people don't matter more than God**. God doesn't expect us to do more than we can realistically do! If we're pushing ourselves too hard, we're probably trying to meet others' expectations, not God's.

"Fear of man will prove to be a snare, but whoever trusts in the LORD is kept safe" (Proverbs 29 v 25).

For Christians, God alone is our Master. Do your best and work your hardest to serve Him. Don't get yourself worked up because of others' expectations.

TREASURE HUNTING

We need to remind ourselves that this life will not last for ever and is not all there is. What a relief! If we know Jesus as our Rescuer, we have an eternity with Him to look forward to. During stressful times, as at any other time, our priority should be serving Him and working for things that are going to last.

Jesus said: *"Store up for yourselves treasures in heaven, where moth and rust do not destroy, and where thieves do not break in and steal. For where your treasure is, there your heart will be also"* (Matthew 6 v 20–21).

It's one thing reading what the Bible says about stress, but it can be a struggle to put it into practice. The best thing you can do is talk to your heavenly Father. Tell Him about your plans for each day, about how you're feeling and what you're worried about. Ask God to show you His priorities and give you the strength you need to serve Him. Hand your stress over to God.

"Cast all your anxiety on him for he cares for you" (1 Peter 5 v 7).

Taken from an article in Don't Panic! *— The Ultimate Exam Survival Kit by Martin Cole and Andrew Roycroft. Available from The Good Book Company website.*

25

18 | EPHESIANS: Big big stuff

Back to Ephesians, where Paul was telling us about God's perfect plans to create a new people. Now Paul moves on to loads of practical advice about how God's people — Christians — should live.

👁 Read Ephesians 4 v 7–10

ENGAGE YOUR BRAIN

▷ Who has given what to who? (v7–8)

Jesus died, was raised back to life and now rules in heaven. He has given believers far more than they deserve — including the ability to serve Him in different ways.

👁 Read verses 11–13

▷ Why is Christian teaching so important?

▷ What's the ultimate goal? (v13)

👁 Read verses 14–16

▷ What do we need to watch out for? (v14)

▷ How can we avoid such dangers? (v15)

▷ How does the church ("the body of Christ") grow? (v16)

God gives His people different abilities to serve Him in different ways. Those who teach us play a big role in building up God's people in truth and love. This leads to unity and maturity. The more we grow in our knowledge of Jesus, the easier we'll be able to avoid crafty false teaching. As we keep talking truth and showing love for each other, Jesus will hold us together and help us to grow.

THINK IT OVER

▷ How can you "speak truth" to people more effectively?

▷ Who do you need to show more love to?

▷ How could your church/youth group be more united?

PRAY ABOUT IT

Thank Jesus for His role in uniting and building up His people. Ask Him to help you grow in faith and understanding.

→ TAKE IT FURTHER

Serving suggestions on page 111.

19 | Spot the difference

What's the difference between Christians and everyone else? Is there any distinction? Does it even matter? Would you say you're any different in the way you live from anyone else?

👁 Read Ephesians 4 v 17–19

ENGAGE YOUR BRAIN

▷ *What does Paul say Christians must do? (v17)*

▷ *Why is this so hard?*

Non-Christians will go on living the way they do. But we're no longer to be like them. Verses 18–19 show us the process at work in unbelievers: they harden their hearts against God... so they can't think right any more... so God turns away from them... so they become self-seeking and immoral — and it's unsatisfying.

Does this ring true to you? Well, it's what we were like, before...

👁 Read verses 20–24

Now see the process that brings a non-Christian to Jesus: you heard of Him (v21)... you were taught the truth (v21)... you threw off your old ways and desires (v22)... and were made new (v23).

That's someone becoming a Christian — God remaking them as a new creation, more like Him.

▷ *What is God's purpose for us? (v24)*

▷ *How would you answer someone who said there's no difference between Christians and everyone else?*

PRAY ABOUT IT

Ask God to help you put off your old sinful ways and desires so you become more righteous and more like Him.

THE BOTTOM LINE

Christians are different.

→ TAKE IT FURTHER

Spot the difference between page 111 and page 1024.

20 Dos and Don'ts

Ever feel like you're coasting as a Christian? That you're not really any different than before? Paul says that's not an option. Living as a Christian means making radical changes to your life.

👁 Read Ephesians 4 v 25–32

ENGAGE YOUR BRAIN

▶ What are the don'ts of Christian living?

v26:

v27:

v28:

v29:

v30:

▶ So what positive things should we do?

v25:

v28:

v29:

v31:

v32:

▶ What reasons are given for living this way?

v25:

v28:

v29:

v32:

GET ON WITH IT

▶ What changes do you need to make in your life?

-
-
-
-

PRAY ABOUT IT

Spend time talking these things over with God.

THE BOTTOM LINE

Living as a Christian means big changes. For the better.

→ TAKE IT FURTHER

DO check out page 111. DON'T forget.

21 | Great impressions

The great thing about Paul's teaching is that he doesn't just dish out commands. He tells us why we should live this way. Here's more in-your-face stuff on Christian lifestyle. Look out!

Read Ephesians 5 v 1–7

ENGAGE YOUR BRAIN

▶ *What are we to do, and why? (v1–2)*

▶ *What specific things does Paul say we need to kick out? (v3–4)*

▶ *What's the incentive for right living in v5–6?*

We're God's children and so should imitate Him in the way we live. Remembering Jesus giving up His life for us should motivate us to live His way. Paul homes in on sexual sin. He says there's no place in a Christian's life for greed or impurity, expecially sexually. And that includes dirty jokes (v4). We should thank God for the gift of sex; not mock it or abuse it. In fact, we should stay away from people who do (v7).

GET ON WITH IT

▶ *What specific sin do you need to kick out of your life?*

▶ *In what ways can you imitate God better?*

Read verses 8–14

▶ *What must Christians do and not do? (v8–11)*

▶ *What are some of the "fruitless deeds of darkness"? (v11)*

Christians have moved from the darkness of sin to new lives in the light of Jesus. So we should live in the light — with nothing to hide. No actions or secret fantasies we'd prefer others not to know about.

PRAY ABOUT IT

Talk to God honestly about the dark things you still cling on to. Ask Him to help you kick them out of your life.

THE BOTTOM LINE

Christians have moved from darkness to light.

→ TAKE IT FURTHER

Follow the light to page 111.

22 Waste of time?

Do you use your time wisely? Do you take every opportunity to live for God? In which areas do you excel and where do you sometimes fail?

Read Ephesians 5 v 15–18

ENGAGE YOUR BRAIN

▶ *Why do we need to use our time wisely? (end of v16)*

▶ *What must we try to do? (v17)*

▶ *What specific advice does Paul give? (v18)*

Christians should be careful how they use their time. We live in evil times, where many people reject God, so we should grab every opportunity to live in a way that brings glory to God. That means making sure our priorities are in line with God's. That's not easy, but the more we read the Bible, the more we understand what God's will is.

One particularly wasteful use of time is getting drunk, which opens us up to all kinds of temptation and sin More on alcohol in *Take it further*). Paul says: Don't fill yourself with booze; be filled with the Holy Spirit...

Read verses 19–20

▶ *What are some of the signs of being filled with the Spirit?*

To be *"filled with the Spirit"* is not a one-off special experience. It's an ongoing privilege that Christians are continually filled with God's Spirit, helping them to live wisely. Signs of being filled with the Spirit include singing together (!), singing to God from our hearts and constantly thanking God for all He's done.

GET ON WITH IT

▶ *How are you at those things?*
▶ *What can you work on?*
▶ *And what about alcohol — how do you need to be more wise with it?*

PRAY ABOUT IT

Talk to God about anything He's challenged you with today.

➡ TAKE IT FURTHER

Still not full? Try page 112.

23 | Marriage = church?

What do you think of marriage? Do you dream of having a fairy tale wedding? Maybe you think it's all a waste of time. Well, Paul has some surprising things to say about marriage, husbands and wives.

👁 Read Ephesians 5 v 21–24

ENGAGE YOUR BRAIN

▷ *What does v22 mean?*

▷ *Why must wives do this? (v24)*

Paul says marriage is a picture of Christ's relationship with His church (all Christians). Believers should adoringly give their lives to serving Jesus, accepting His authority. And wives should accept the authority of their husbands, as an expression of unselfish love. But don't assume that husbands get an easy ride...

👁 Read verses 25–33

▷ *How must husbands treat their wives? (v25, v28)*

▷ *What goals should a husband have? (v26–27)*

Husbands must show the self-giving, sacrificial, purposeful love that Jesus did for His church. Their wives can become all that God wants them to be. Great, eh? A husband should love and look after His wife in the same way he cares for himself — instinctively and naturally — because she's part of him now (v31). Amazingly, Christ also counts His people as His own body and He cares for them, providing for them. Both sets of relationships are incredibly intimate.

PRAY ABOUT IT

Thank Jesus for His love and commitment to His church — Christians. Spend time praying for married couples you know: that they would show this same kind of inseparable love and devotion to each other.

→ TAKE IT FURTHER

More man and woman stuff on page 112.

24 | Home, work

If you're a Christian, your faith should have a big impact on every aspect of your life. That includes home life and work. Which is great news for parents and bosses!

👁 Read Ephesians 6 v 1–4

ENGAGE YOUR BRAIN

▷ *What's it mean to honour your parents when you're at home?*

▷ *What about once you've left home?*

▷ *What big responsibility do parents have? (v4)*

None of us likes being told what to do. But Paul tells us to obey our parents — it's the right thing to do (v1), God commands us to do it (v2), and it's good for us (v3). This teaching even applies for the worst parents. The Bible teaches us that obedient children are happy children! (v3)

👁 Read verses 5–9

▷ *How were slaves to behave? (v5–8) Why?*

▷ *What must masters do? (v9) And why?*

▷ *How could these same principles change the way you work?*

Think of the way you honour and treat Jesus. We're to obey our earthly masters in the same way! Radical stuff. It's not so they think we're great (v6) — we're doing it to serve the Lord (v7).

GET ON WITH IT

▷ *How do you need to treat your parents differently?*
▷ *What about other people with authority over you?*
▷ *And how will you transform the way you work?*

PRAY ABOUT IT

There's no denying it — you've got loads to talk to God about today.

THE BOTTOM LINE

Honour your parents, work for God.

→ TAKE IT FURTHER

Collect your homework on page 112.

25 Armour of God

Paul says: Be pure, united and strong in your faith. Great — let's do that! Then Paul reminds us of our terrifying enemies, and suddenly we no longer feel quite so confident...

Read Ephesians 6 v 10–18

ENGAGE YOUR BRAIN

▷ What opposition do believers face? (v11–12)

▷ What must we do? (v10, v13)

The devil is real, evil, unseen, powerful and cunning. Making us think he doesn't exist is his biggest con, followed by the one about him being a joker with a pitchfork. But Jesus defeated him by the cross and broke his power, and one day will finally wipe him out. More great news is that we can grab God's protection against the devil and any opposition...

Read Ephesians 6 v 14–18

▷ What six things does God equip us with, ready for battle?

▷ Which is the only piece of armour used as a weapon? (v17)

▷ What else must Christians do constantly? (v18)

These pieces of armour are all different aspects of the gospel —

the good news of what God has done for us in Jesus. We're to stand firm against opposition, using...

- **truth** — to cling onto against the lies we'll hear
- **righteousness** — living lives that show we're right with God
- **the gospel** — relying on what Jesus has done for us, and sharing the good news with others
- **faith** — trusting in God, no matter what we face
- **salvation** — remembering that Jesus has rescued us, not doubting whose side we're on
- **word of God** — with the Holy Spirit's help, the Bible is our weapon against evil, doubt and temptation.

PRAY ABOUT IT

Thank God that He equips us perfectly to face any opposition. Ask Him to help you put on your armour and go into battle for Him. And pray for other Christians you know.

➡ TAKE IT FURTHER

Prepare for battle on page 112.

33

26 Pray hard

Yesterday we tried on God's armour, which we need to survive the battles we face as Christians. Something else that's vital for God's army is prayer.

Read Ephesians 6 v 18–20

ENGAGE YOUR BRAIN
▷ *When is it right to pray? (v18)*
▷ *What kind of prayers should we pray? (v18)*
▷ *Who should we pray for? (v18–19)*

God's army is no place for half-hearted occasional prayer. We should pray in every situation, in loads of different ways, about anything and everything. We should especially pray for Christians ("*saints*") and for people who spread the gospel, as Paul did. Pray that they will speak about Jesus fearlessly.

Read verses 21–24

▷ *Why did Paul send Tychicus to Ephesus? (v22)*

Another thing that helps us stand firm as Christians is encouragement. We can encourage each other with stories of God at work in our lives, as Tychicus was doing. And we can encourage people by letting them know we're praying for them. Look at Paul's prayer in v23–24: what greater things can we ask for people we care about? Peace, love and grace.

GET ON WITH IT
▷ *Who will you encourage this week?*
▷ *How will you do it?*

PRAY ABOUT IT
Spend longer in prayer today. Make your prayer...
• about things you don't often pray about, all kinds of situations
• in different ways, not just the same old words
• for Christians you know who share the gospel
• for Christian friends, that they will know God's love, grace and peace.

THE BOTTOM LINE
Pray hard and encourage each other.

→ TAKE IT FURTHER
Final word on Ephesians — page 112.

27 | NUMBERS: Counting on God

Back to Moses and the Israelites in Numbers. The 40 years of wandering in the desert are nearly at an end, but what's this? Surely the people can't be grumbling again?

👁 Read Numbers 20 v 1–13

ENGAGE YOUR BRAIN

- ▷ *How does this chapter begin and end? (v1 and v29)*
- ▷ *What tone does this give to the events in the chapter as a whole?*
- ▷ *Why are v2–4 so disappointing?*
- ▷ *Compare v7–13 with Exodus 17 v 1–7. What are the similarities? What are the differences?*
- ▷ *What is the sad outcome for Moses? (v12)*

Maybe God is angry with Moses because he loses his cool with the Israelites; maybe it's because he disobeys God's instructions. The important thing is that he didn't trust and honour God (v12).

In the earlier incident in Exodus 17 v 6, Moses is told to strike the rock in order to release God's grace. But on this occasion, he is not told to do that. So by lashing out at the rock he shows disrespect for God.

PRAY ABOUT IT

Have there been occasions recently where you have shown disrespect towards God? Using His name as a swear word? Taking His forgiveness for granted, and deliberately sinning anyway? Talk to Him now and ask for His forgiveness.

👁 Read verses 14–29

Edom was descended from Esau, Jacob's (AKA Israel's) brother, so was a distant relative of the Israelite nation.

- ▷ *Why is Edom's response so disappointing? (v14–21)*
- ▷ *Why does Aaron die now? (v24)*
- ▷ *How would you sum up the mood of this whole chapter?*

THE BOTTOM LINE

Earthly leaders ultimately fail. Only Jesus Christ is the perfect leader, King and High Priest.

→ TAKE IT FURTHER

Something more positive can be found on page 112.

28 | Snakes alive!

Some positives now as the Israelites begin to defeat their enemies and march closer to the promised land — but it's not all straightforward. As always, the inner problem of their own hearts is far greater than any enemy armies.

👁 Read Numbers 21 v 1–9

ENGAGE YOUR BRAIN

▶ Why are the Israelites successful against the Canaanites? (v2–3)

▶ What is the issue (again) in v4–5?

▶ Why is v5 such an awful thing to say?

PRAY ABOUT IT

Be honest — do you ever moan about what God has graciously given you? Your parents? Your church? Spend some time thanking Him instead.

▶ What is God's response — firstly in judgment and then in mercy? (v6–9)

▶ What does this tell us about God?

👁 Skim read verses 10–35

▶ Find some positives about the events in the rest of the chapter (eg: v17, v25, v32, v35).

Chapter 22 v 1 tells us that the Israelites had reached the banks of the Jordan river — they were almost there; the promised land!

▶ What are you expecting to happen next? Why?

▶ What do you know about the Israelites?

▶ What do you know about God and His promises?

Things are improving — we're seeing a growing dependence on God in prayer (v2) and victory (v3), where there was a crushing defeat 35 years earlier.

THINK IT OVER

Those who trusted what God said, turned to the rescue He provided (v9). The same offer is open to us through Jesus. Have you accepted it yet?

→ TAKE IT FURTHER

Snake your way over to page 113.

29 | Prophet profit

Balak, king of Moab, was scared by God's people's march towards the promised land. So he decided to "rent a curse" from the biggest name in pagan prophets — Balaam. But things don't exactly go according to plan...

👁 Read Numbers 22 v 1–20

ENGAGE YOUR BRAIN

▶ *What is worrying Balak? (v2–4)*

▶ *What does he want from Balaam?*

▶ *How does God intervene? (v9–12)*

▶ *Is this the end of the story? (v14–19)*

▶ *What do you think Balaam wants? (clue: v7 and v18)*

Balaam obviously doesn't take God speaking to him very seriously. After all, the fake pagan gods he's used to are easy to manipulate for his own personal gain, so maybe this one will change his mind too for the right price.

👁 Read verses 21–41

▶ *What is God teaching Balaam about who He is?*

▶ *How does Balaam eventually respond?*

▶ *Who is the real donkey in this story?*

Does it ever annoy you when you see people trying to use God or manipulate Christianity for their own (often financial) benefit? Take comfort from the fact that God knows exactly what these sorts of people are up to and will hold them responsible.

TALK IT OVER

Does it ever look as though Christians are at the mercy of the world around us? Chat with another Christian about ways in which you can seem outnumbered and overpowered by unbelievers. Then look at Numbers 22 v 12. How does that help you to see God's perspective?

THE BOTTOM LINE

You can't manipulate God.

→ TAKE IT FURTHER

Profit and loss on page 113.

30 Don't be a donkey

An almost comical turn of events now as Balak hustles Balaam round various viewpoints to curse God's people, only to meet with total failure — and worse, blessing — at every turn!

Read Numbers 23v1–24v13

ENGAGE YOUR BRAIN

▷ *Sum up events using the table below:*

	23v1-2	23v13-26	23v27-24v11
Preparations made			
God's message about Israel via Balaam			
Balak's response			

▷ What do we learn about God from 23 v 19?
▷ What do we learn about Balak and Balaam?

PRAY ABOUT IT

God is in charge and His promises always come true. Thank Him for that now — perhaps mentioning specific examples from the Bible that encourage you (eg: John 3 v 16, James 5 v 20).

THE BOTTOM LINE

What God says, happens.

→ TAKE IT FURTHER

More info on God's enemies on page 113.

31 | The destroyer

Operation Curse Israel had been a remarkable failure, but God has one more thing to say through Balaam. Balak won't like it...

👁 Read Numbers 24 v 14–25

ENGAGE YOUR BRAIN
▷ *Who does God promise will come? (v17, v19)*

▷ *What will this person do?*

This promised king is not new (see Genesis 17 v 16, 35 v 11 and 49 v 10). But who is he?

👁 Read 2 Samuel 8 v 1–14

👁 Read 1 Corinthians 15v25–26

While David was a great king who defeated many of Israel's enemies (just as Balaam predicted), Jesus is the ultimate King. The one who will rule for ever.

PRAY ABOUT IT
Read Philippians 2 v 9–11
Pray for people you know who are currently God's enemies. Pray that they would willingly bow to Jesus as their King now, rather than being forced to do so later, when He returns as Judge.

SHARE IT
Can you talk to someone about what an amazing King Jesus is this week? You could start with how He has changed your life.

THE BOTTOM LINE
God's King will destroy all His enemies.

→ TAKE IT FURTHER
More about the King on page 113.

32   Seduction technique

Sometimes it's not outright opposition like Balak's which poses the most danger to God's people. Often subtle distraction can be far more deadly.

Read Numbers 25 v 1–18

ENGAGE YOUR BRAIN

▷ *Who was behind the actions of the women in this story? (see 31 v 15–16)*

▷ *How did these women harm the Israelites? (v1–3)*

▷ *Why is God so angry? Think back to the Ten Commandments (Exodus 20 v 1–3)*

GET ON WITH IT

Are you being seduced away from God at the moment? Look carefully at your life — are those films, TV shows, websites, books or magazines helping you to stay close to God or are they enticing you away? If they're a bad influence, get rid of them!

▷ *What is your initial response to Phineas's actions? (v6–8)*

▷ *Why?*

▷ *How does God assess what he did? (v11–13)*

Who do you relate to in this story? Naturally we're all like Zimri and Cozbi. But instead of us getting speared, Jesus takes the spear instead of us (see John 19 v 34). Not just for sexual sin, but for all sins. Like Phineas, one man makes atonement for the sins of the people, but unlike him, Jesus takes the punishment upon Himself.

PRAY ABOUT IT

Thank God that Jesus' death means every single one of your sins can be forgiven.

THE BOTTOM LINE

Jesus took the spear instead of us.

TAKE IT FURTHER

A little more is on page 113.

33 Time for a recount

Back to the numbers game now. Loads of names here, but try to spot what has changed since last census (back in chapter 1).

👁 Read chapter 26

ENGAGE YOUR BRAIN

▶ *Why are the people being counted (v2)?*

▶ *How does the total number here compare to the first census 40 years earlier? (compare v51 to 1 v 46)*

▶ *What does that suggest about:*
a) Israel's progress over 40 years?
b) God's promise to make His people as numerous as the stars?

God's promises have been delayed but not stopped by His people's sin. Here they are, finally on the border of the promised land and, despite appearances, the 40 years in the desert have taught them some valuable lessons. (And did you notice v33? Keep it in mind for tomorrow.)

▶ *What do v63–65 remind us about God and His people?*

▶ *What lessons do you think they have learned over the past 40 years?*

PRAY ABOUT IT

Thank God that He is patient with us. Why not use Exodus 34 v 6–7 and Psalm 103 as a basis for your prayers?

THE BOTTOM LINE

God's promises cannot be hindered, even by our sin.

→ TAKE IT FURTHER

To take it further, count all the way up to 113.

34 | Here come the girls

The story of Zelophehad's daughters begins and ends this final section of Numbers. (Remember them from 26 v 33?) But why is their predicament so important? Read on!

👁 Read Numbers 27 v 1–11

ENGAGE YOUR BRAIN

▶ What problem do Zelophehad's daughters face? (v3–4)

▶ How are you expecting Moses and God to respond?

▶ What is God's reply? (v7–11)

▶ Why do you think He takes their case so seriously?

Do you remember the problem 40 years previously when the Israelites first reached the borders of the promised land? Intimidated by the size of the people living there, they despised God's promises and rejected the land He was giving them. But now, Zelophehad's daughters really want their part of the inheritance. They take God's promises seriously and they really value the land God is giving to Israel — hooray!

👁 Read Numbers 36 v 1–11

▶ What are the relatives of Zelophehad's daughters worried about? (v2–4)

▶ Does God take their concern seriously? (v5–9)

▶ Again, what does this show about God's attitude to the land?

▶ How do Zelophehad's daughters respond? (v10–12)

What a great way to finish the book — God's people will soon arrive in God's place. And they have the right attitude of faith in God's promises and obedience to His commands!

GET ON WITH IT

How can you show by your actions that you take God's promises seriously today? In what you say? How you behave? The choices you make?

PRAY ABOUT IT

Ask God to help you trust and obey Him today.

THE BOTTOM LINE

Take God's promises seriously.

→ TAKE IT FURTHER

Grab a little extra on page 113.

35 | Out for the count

Poor old Moses — he almost made it, but not quite. But God's rescue and promises are not dependent on this human leader.

👁 Read Numbers 27 v 12–23

ENGAGE YOUR BRAIN

▷ Why would Moses not make it into the promised land? (v14)

▷ What is Moses most concerned about? (v16–17)

▷ What will make Joshua a suitable leader (v18–20)?

Seems a bit hard on Moses, getting to see the promised land but not actually entering it. But God keeps His word and Moses faces the consequences of his sin, just as everyone else does.

GET ON WITH IT

Did v17 sound a bit familiar? Check out Matthew 9 v 35–37 — think of the people you know who are lost without Jesus. Pray for an opportunity to introduce them to Jesus, our perfect Shepherd.

👁 Skim read chapters 28–30

There is a lot of repetition here of laws and festivals we've already seen in Exodus and Leviticus. But Moses wants to remind the people of how God has rescued them and how they should relate to Him as they prepare for a new beginning.

▷ What are we reminded about the Israelites and also about God in these verses?
28 v 1–15:
28 v 16–25:
28 v 26–31:
29 v 1–6:
29 v 7–11:
29 v 12–40:
30 v 1–16:

PRAY ABOUT IT

Turn some of the things you've mentioned above into prayer — thanking God for all His good gifts, for His forgiveness, and for Jesus.

THE BOTTOM LINE

Jesus is the perfect leader.

→ TAKE IT FURTHER

You can count on page 114.

36 | Last orders

What might you expect Moses' last mission for God to be? Some more teaching? A special fast, maybe? Or a violent massacre?

👁 Read Numbers 31 v 1–18

ENGAGE YOUR BRAIN
- ▷ What did God command? (v2–3)
- ▷ Were they ruthless enough with God's enemies? (v7–12)
- ▷ Really? (v13–18)

Seems pretty harsh? But look again at v16 — Balaam and the women involved were responsible for turning God's people against Him (25 v 16–18). And to be fair, the women who weren't involved didn't face God's anger (v18).

PRAY ABOUT IT
Do you find things like this hard to read? Being on the receiving end of God's anger is not a good place to be. But if He is truly God, He has the right to judge. The amazing thing is that He chooses to show mercy. Read **Romans 5 v 6–11** and use it to help you pray.

👁 Skim Numbers 32 v 1–42
- ▷ What do the Reubenites and Gadites want? (v5)
- ▷ Why is this potentially disastrous? (v6–15)
- ▷ How do the Reubenites and Gadites assure Moses they are not rebelling against God? (v16–19)

They get what they want and, to be fair, they do stick to their word. But in settling for what looks materially attractive, the Reubenites and Gadites (and the half tribe of Manasseh) show a lack of spiritual wisdom — they are disregarding God's promises.

GET ON WITH IT
Ever tempted to go for something which is more attractive here and now than hold on to God's promises? That non-Christian girlfriend or boyfriend? A Sunday job which pays well but means you miss church? A night out having fun getting drunk with your mates rather than going to youth group? Need to change?

→ TAKE IT FURTHER
War words on page 114.

37 | Numbering off

As we reach the end of Numbers there's some looking back and looking forward to be done — both at where the Israelites have come from and what they're heading to!

👁 **Read Numbers 33 v 1–49**
to see how the Israelites got to this point.

👁 **Read verses 50–56**

ENGAGE YOUR BRAIN
▷ What is the promise Israel is reminded of here?
▷ What is the warning?

👁 **Read Numbers 34 v 1–29**
to see what God gave to the Israelites.

👁 **Speed read chapter 35**
▷ What was the job of the Levites?
▷ Why were they spread out through the land?

▷ What do all the rules about killing (accidental or not) remind us about God? (v33–34)

PRAY ABOUT IT
God is a pure and holy God, but He also wants a relationship with sinful people. Thank Him that Jesus taking our punishment on the cross has made this possible.

THE BOTTOM LINE
God is faithful
and generous.

ISRAEL

→ **TAKE IT FURTHER**
Find your way to
page 114.

● MOAB

● RAMASES

● GOSHEN
● SUCCOTH

● MIGDOL

● PUNON

● KADESH

EGYPT

● MARAH
● ELIM

DESERT OF SIN

● HAZEROTH

● DOPHKAH

RED SEA

RED SEA

● REPHDIM ● MT. SINAI

45

Why does God allow suffering?

Each issue in TRICKY, we tackle those mind-bendingly difficult questions that confuse us all. This time, we ask the controversial question: **Why does God let bad stuff happen?**

One of the biggest barriers that gets in between people and God is the issue of suffering. *"How can a God of love allow so much evil and pain to exist?"* It's not unusual when someone loses a relative to cancer to hear them say: *"I can't believe in a God who would let that happen."* So why does God allow suffering in the world?

WE IGNORE GOD

It's not a new problem. Even in Old Testament times, a psalm writer said: *"Why, O Lord, do you stand far off? Why do you hide yourself in times of trouble?"* (Psalm 10 v 1). The difficult truth is that the suffering in the world is our fault. God tells us not to murder, steal, tell lies or be jealous of other people (Exodus 20 v 13–17). Think how much suffering, violence, war and famine would be cut out if people obeyed God and lived for Him instead of themselves.

> The great news is that God has done something about pain.

God tells us to love other people, and not put ourselves first. He tells us to help the people around us (Galatians 6 v 9–10). He tells us to look after people who are sad, hungry, lonely or poor (Luke 10 v 30–37, Matthew 25 v 34–46). If everyone obeyed God and helped out people worse off than them, there would be no poverty in the world. But people are greedy. They put themselves first. Get rich. Be comfortable. Have a nice, easy life. While people starve.

God didn't create humans as robots, who always do the right thing. He gave us the responsability to choose the way we live. To live for Him or for ourselves. To obey Him or do what most pleases us. To be selfish or put others first. Sadly, we all choose ourselves, and ignore God, which is why the world is in such

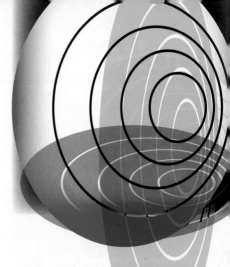

a bad way. We ask: *"Why doesn't God stop all this war, poverty and suffering?"* And God could say: *"I created a perfect world, with no sin, greed or violence but humans messed it up. Why don't YOU do something about it?"*

We can't. We're all slaves to sin. Yet despite our sin and rebellion — and all the suffering we've caused — God sent His Son Jesus to rescue us from our sin slavery.

NO EASY ANSWERS

But what about suffering that isn't a result of human choices — earthquakes, floods, babies born with disabilities? All these things are signs of the fallen world we live in. At the start of Genesis, humans lived in a perfect world with God. But they chose to sin, and the result was a fallen, imperfect world. Human sin has caused suffering in the world.

The Bible book of Job is all about seemingly unfair suffering. There were no easy answers for Job. Sometimes we just don't know why bad things happen. We can't expect to understand God's plans and why He allows suffering to continue. He's totally different from us (Isaiah 55 v 8). He's also sovereign — that means He's in charge of everything. He's God, He can do anything He wishes. That would be a scary thought if we didn't know that God is so trustworthy (2 Samuel 7 v 28). He always does the right thing. We may not understand at the time why bad things

are allowed to happen, but we can be sure that God loves us and will always do what's best for us. Paul tells us that *"in all things God works for the good of those who love him"* (Romans 8 v 28). We may not always see it at the time, but God could be using a time of suffering to strengthen us and bring us closer to Him.

GOD'S RESPONSE

It's a mistake to think that God happily leaves people to wallow in the suffering of the world. The great news is that God has done something about our pain. Jesus suffered horrifically and died so that we can be forgiven. God offers to end our suffering for ever. Anyone who trusts in Jesus' death on their behalf will one day live with Him for all eternity in a place where there will be no sin, suffering or sadness!

The fact that God sent His only Son to suffer and die and rescue us from sin is overwhelming evidence that God DOES care for us and love us.

Luke

Walking with Jesus

Who would you most like to meet? If you could go for a walk with them one afternoon, what would you ask them? What tips would you want from them about how to approach life?

In Luke 12–18, God's Son, Jesus, has got more than an afternoon with His friends and the crowds who followed Him — but He is still on limited time. Jesus is walking to Jerusalem, and He knows that when He gets there He won't be placed on a throne; He'll die on a cross in agony.

So in this section of Luke's historical account of His life, Jesus is telling those around Him why it's worth following Him, and what it'll be like to live that way.

He does this in a variety of ways: meeting people, answering questions, telling stories, reacting to events. But all the time He's answering these two questions:

Why's it worth following Jesus?

What does it mean to follow Jesus?

You're 2,000 years too late to walk with Jesus to Jerusalem; but thanks to Luke you can still be part of each scene, and listen to Jesus speak to you about your life.

Maybe you're still working out for yourself who Jesus is. The crowd around Him were trying to do that too — so over the next few weeks you'll have the chance each day to see for yourself.

And if you're already a friend of Jesus, dive in and find out how the Lord of life tells you to approach your own life.

38 | Don't don't don't

It's annoying when people say: "Don't do that!" without giving a good reason. Here, Jesus has three "don'ts" — but gives us three massive reasons why.

👁 **Read Luke 12 v 1–3**

ENGAGE YOUR BRAIN

▷ *Jesus and the Pharisees often disagreed. What's their problem according to Jesus? (v1)*

It's easy to be a hypocritical Christian — to say we follow Jesus but then not bother when it gets hard.

▷ *Why can't we get away with that? (v2–3)*

Jesus is describing the day He returns, when everything, even what's currently hidden in our hearts, will be "made known". Ouch!

👁 **Read verses 4–7**

▷ *What's the next don't? (v4)*

If we care what other people think, we'll be afraid of standing up for Jesus. But the worst a man can do is kill you (v4). But Jesus has the power to send people to hell. We should be more concerned about what Jesus

thinks of us than what people do!

👁 **Read verses 8–12**

▷ *What's true if we stand up for Jesus? (v8)*

SHARE IT

▷ *How can you speak out more for Jesus?*

▷ *What's the great news when you do make a stand? (v11–12)*

PRAY ABOUT IT

What's on your mind after today's study? Talk to God about it.

THE BOTTOM LINE

When He returns, Jesus will reveal everything, send people to hell, and welcome those who stood up for Him: so don't be hypocritical, don't be afraid of people and don't disown Jesus.

→ **TAKE IT FURTHER**

Confused by v10? Try page 114.

39 Fat cat fate

How far ahead do you plan? In the next few chunks of Luke's Gospel, Jesus deals with matters like money, clothes and stuff. And He tells a story about a guy who planned his early retirement.

Read Luke 12 v 13–21

ENGAGE YOUR BRAIN

▷ Jesus has been talking about how to have eternal life with Him when He returns – but what's this guy more worried about? (v13)

▷ What is the man in Jesus' story most worried about? (v16–18)

He's not just trying to put some food on the table — he's got so many possessions he has to build huge barns to put them in!

▷ What's he looking forward to? (v19)

▷ What does God think of him? And why? (v20–21)

▷ What point is Jesus making? (end of v15)

Both the man talking to Jesus and the guy in the parable are focusing on storing up things for themselves for this life. What should their priority be? (v21)

THINK IT THROUGH

▷ How should Christians think about wealth?

▷ Should our prayers focus more on asking Jesus to give us what we want, or asking Him to help us follow Him?

PRAY ABOUT IT

Jesus, Help me to concentrate not on having money, which will buy good things now, but on having a relationship with you, which will bring me eternal life. Amen.

THE BOTTOM LINE

Make sure you're focused on the riches of eternal life which Jesus offers, not on the short-lived wealth of what this world offers!

→ TAKE IT FURTHER

More on money matters — page 114.

40 | Don't worry, be happy

**Do you trust in God?
And do you worry about stuff?
Jesus says trusting God and worrying
about life don't go together.**

👁 Read Luke 12 v 22–31

ENGAGE YOUR BRAIN

▷ *What does God do for ravens? (v24)*

▷ *Are God's people more or less valuable to Him than birds? (v24)*

▷ *So what will God do for them?*

▷ *So, what shouldn't we do? (v22)*

▷ *What should we live for? (v31)*

The opposite of faith is… worrying! If I worry about something, I'm not trusting that God can provide, or that God knows what I need, or that God my Father loves me. Worrying shows that in my heart I trust in myself, not God — which is crazy! When I want to worry, I need to turn in trust to our amazing, all-providing God.

THINK IT THROUGH

▷ *What's one thing you worry about which you need to trust your Father God for?*

When you worry about that thing, find ways to remind yourself that God's in control, or that He knows what you need and that He loves you.

👁 Read verses 32–34

▷ *Since God gives us everything we need, including eternal life in "the kingdom" (v32), what should we do? (v33)*

▷ *If I concentrate on having eternal treasure instead of being rich now, what does that show? (v34)*

THE BOTTOM LINE

Trusting in the God who provides for us and knows us means we don't need to worry and can be generous.

PRAY ABOUT IT

Ask God to help you turn to Him in trust next time you want to worry.

→ TAKE IT FURTHER

Worried? Try page 115.

41

Get ready

Your parents leave you to an empty house. Do you...
- **throw a party and trash it?**
- **laze around and let it get really messy?**
- **enjoy it, but make sure you're ready for their return?**

👁 Read Luke 12 v 35–40

ENGAGE YOUR BRAIN

▶ *These servants have an empty house... what's the sensible thing to do? (v38)*

▶ *What will the master then do for them? (second half of v37)*

We live in Jesus' world. He's not here right now — He's in heaven. It's like having an empty house — what will we do with it?

▶ *What does Jesus, the "Son of Man", say we must do? (v40)*

▶ *Why?*

The only way to be ready for a thief (v39) is to be ready all the time — thieves don't say when they'll come! Jesus hasn't told us when He'll come back to His world, so the only way to be ready for Him is to be ready all the time.

So, how can we show we're ready?

👁 Read verses 41–48

The manager could show he was ready by looking after the other servants. We show we're ready for Jesus' return by looking after His people. We can all pray for and encourage our Christian friends. If we're doing that, we're showing we're ready for Jesus' return to His world!

People who know Jesus' demands but do nothing will be punished more than those who don't know Jesus at all (v47).

PRAY ABOUT IT

Ask God to show you how to serve Him and care for other believers.

→ TAKE IT FURTHER

Get ready for more on page 115.

42 | Our place in history

We live in the 21st century. In the internet age. In the postmodern era. And, much more importantly, we live between two massive markers in time...

👁 **Read Luke 12 v 49–56**

ENGAGE YOUR BRAIN

▶ *What did Jesus say He had come to bring? (v49)*

▶ *What did He have to do before that? (v50)*

Two strange images in those verses! The first is talking about Jesus' judgment, when He will "burn up" everything that isn't to be part of His perfect world. The second is one of the ways Jesus talked about His death on the cross.

So these are the two markers in time which we live between — Jesus dying to give His people a place in His perfect world; and Jesus returning to burn up everything that doesn't have a place there. We need to remember this and live in a way that shows it (v56).

Question is — what happens between these two markers in time?

▶ *What will there and what won't there be? (v51)*

The world, even families, will be divided between those who follow Jesus and those who don't (v52–53).

👁 **Read verses 57–59**

This guy needs to make friends with his enemy before he gets to court and a judgment — or he'll go to prison. Jesus has already reminded us that He will come in judgment.

▶ *Who do people need to become friends with before that day?*

PRAY ABOUT IT

We live between Jesus' death and Jesus' return — we need to make sure we're friends with God, and expect hard times, not peace. Pray for those you know who aren't Christians. And ask God to help you when people turn against you.

➔ **TAKE IT FURTHER**

More about all this on page 115.

43 | Disaster strikes

Sometimes on the news there's an earthquake or a tsunami, a war or a massacre, and we're reminded that death is real. How should we respond?

Read Luke 13 v 1–5

ENGAGE YOUR BRAIN

In Jesus' day, if people died in a horrible or unfortunate way, people often responded by saying: *"Ah, they must have done something really bad. That's why they've died like that."*

▶ What does Jesus think of that idea?

▶ In fact, what should another person's death remind us of? (v3, v5)

Because we're all sinners, no one deserves to live forever. Everyone deserves to die just as much as everyone else. The only way to live forever is to turn back to God, to repent.

Read verses 6–9

▶ What does the owner of the useless fig tree tell the man who takes care of it to do? (v7)

▶ What does the man ask for? (v8)

▶ The fig tree represents people who won't turn back to God — what's the warning for these people? (v8–9)

THINK IT OVER

Perhaps you've never actually repented, never turned away from living for yourself and turned back to God. Why not do that now and avoid losing eternal life?

SHARE IT

How does this help you to talk about Christianity next time your friends are talking about a terrible disaster?

THE BOTTOM LINE

Death should remind us that the only way to have life beyond our death is to have turned back to God.

→ TAKE IT FURTHER

Why do disasters happen?
Take it further on page 115.

44 | Jesus vs religion

TV news often ends with a happy story to cheer you up. Then a news summary. Then the commercials. The next bit from Luke shares that pattern. A miraculous story. Then a summary. (OK, so maybe no commercials.)

👁 **Read Luke 13 v 10–17**

ENGAGE YOUR BRAIN

▷ *How did the woman understandably react? (v13)*

▷ *How did the synagogue leader feel, and why? (v14)*

Two very different reactions. The woman who had been broken praised God for healing her; the synagogue leader was furious about broken religious rules. He was wrong. God had told His people to rest one day a week; but He'd never told them not to help people on that day!

▷ *What point is Jesus making in v15–16?*

Jesus reminds us that to enjoy real "rest" — the security and joy of a relationship with God — we need to let Jesus set us free from our sin, rather than thinking that we can earn it by keeping rules.

Going to church, trying to be good — none of it will gain us eternal life. Only Jesus can give it to us.

THINK IT OVER

▷ *What can you praise God for doing in your life?*

▷ *Are there any ways in which you can be like the synagogue ruler, relying on rules to get you right with God?*

THE BOTTOM LINE

Only Jesus can give us the "rest" of eternity with God. We can't earn it.

PRAY ABOUT IT

Thank God that Jesus heals the broken so they can praise God.

→ TAKE IT FURTHER

Verses 18–21 are on page 116.

45 | Best party ever!

The most incredible party's about to start — but will you even get through the door to enjoy it?

Read Luke 13 v 22–30

ENGAGE YOUR BRAIN

▷ *Where is Jesus going? (v22)*

▷ *What will happen there? (Flick back to Luke 9 v 22.)*

▷ *There's a party on — but what will happen to 'many'? (v24–25)*

▷ *These people assume they're the houseowner's friends — but what does he say? (v27)*

▷ *Verse 28 tells us what the "party" is. Where will Abraham, Isaac, Jacob and the prophets be?*

You can't just assume you're Jesus' friend. Many people think if they go to church, or pray, or come from a Christian family, Jesus will let them into God's kingdom. They're in for a shock when He returns and closes the door on them!

Jesus says instead of assuming you're His friend, *"Make every effort to enter through the narrow door."* (v24) OK! Err… what does that actually mean?

▷ *Remember v22. Jesus is walking towards His death. How easy will it be to be one of His followers?*

Following Jesus leads to a place in God's kingdom — but it will sometimes mean being "last" in life (v30). We need to make "every effort" to keep going.

THINK IT OVER

▷ *Have you repented and turned to Jesus for forgiveness?*
▷ *Know anyone who thinks they're all right with God but haven't faced up to their sin?*
▷ *What can you say to them?*
▷ *What will you pray for them right now?*

→ TAKE IT FURTHER

Turn to page 116 for more.

46 | Fox and hens

OK, so the way to perfect, eternal life is to follow Jesus through the narrow door. So everyone will fall into line behind Him. Won't they?

👁 **Read Luke 13 v 31–33**

ENGAGE YOUR BRAIN

▷ What do some Pharisees come to warn Jesus about? (v31)

▷ Is Jesus willing to change His plans just because Herod doesn't like Him? (v32)

▷ What does this tell us about Jesus?

👁 **Read verses 34–35**

▷ Who is Jesus now talking to? (v34)

▷ This was the capital city of Israel, where God's people, the Jews, lived. What does Jesus long to do? (v34)

He wants to pick them up and carry them through the narrow door!

▷ Why doesn't He? (end of v34)

▷ So what will happen to them instead?

THINK IT THROUGH

You'd expect the Jews, God's people, and Herod, a king of God's people, to be the first in line to follow Jesus through the narrow door. But they're not willing — they'd rather kill God's messengers than humbly listen to them.

▷ How's this a warning to us today?

PRAY ABOUT IT

Lord Jesus, thank you that you gather your people together and lead them through the narrow door to eternal life. Help me to be humble enough to be willing to let you do this for me, and never to think I know better than you.

THE BOTTOM LINE

God's true people are those who humbly listen and closely follow Jesus.

→ **TAKE IT FURTHER**

Don't be outfoxed, try page 116.

47 | Food for thought

The Pharisees think Jesus won't fit through their narrow door. But when they invite Him to a dinner party, they soon realise the shoe is on the other foot.

👁 Read Luke 14 v 1–9

Jesus is being "carefully watched" (v1) by His enemies. But they won't change His plans — He'll still heal people (v2–4). When Jesus notices how people position themselves and try to look good (v7), He tells them how those who are following Him through the narrow door should behave.

👁 Read verses 10–14

ENGAGE YOUR BRAIN

🔘 *Where does Jesus tell these important religious leaders to sit? (v10)*

🔘 *Why? (v11)*

🔘 *What does He say to the host about who he should invite? (v13)*

🔘 *When will they be rewarded? (v14)*

🔘 *If you spend your time doing things for important and wealthy people, when do you get your reward? (v12)*

🔘 *The world says we need to put ourselves forward and make sure we gain rewards in life. What does Jesus say?*

The *"resurrection of the righteous"* is talking about when Jesus returns to raise all believers to eternal life with Him. We shouldn't look for rewards now, God will reward us eventually. And we should value everyone, not just the richest, coolest or most important people. We should live for our eternal life to come, not for small rewards and popularity now.

PRAY ABOUT IT

Ask God to show you how you can serve those in need. Ask Him to give you the humility not to look for a reward now. Ask Him to give you an eternal perspective on life.

→ TAKE IT FURTHER

Dessert is on page 116.

48 RSVP

We've seen that some people won't get through the narrow door and will be shut out of God's kingdom. Why?

👁 **Read Luke 14 v 15–24**

ENGAGE YOUR BRAIN

▶ *Any ideas what this guy means? (v15)*

▶ *What does God want? (v16-17, v23)*

▶ *What happens when God invites people into His kingdom? (v18–20)*

▶ *How good are these excuses? (v18–20)*

Just take the first excuse in v18. It's rubbish! If you buy a field, you look at it before you buy it, not after! And if you want to see it again, it'll still be there tomorrow; it won't move!

▶ *How does God respond to people turning down His free invitation to come to His banquet in His kingdom? (v21)*

▶ *What is the result of them making excuses? (v24)*

God invites us to His kingdom — His Son Jesus offers to take us there through the narrow door. But not everyone goes. Many people turn down the invitation.

▶ *What excuses have you heard for rejecting Jesus?*

PRAY IT THROUGH

Thank God for His invitation to His kingdom. If you've not yet responded to His invitation, now is the time. Pray for friends who keep making excuses.

➡ **TAKE IT FURTHER**

No excuses... turn to page 116.

TOOLBOX

Genre

One of the main ambitions of **engage** is to encourage you to dive into God's word and be able to handle it and understand it more. Each issue, TOOLBOX gives you tips, tools and advice for wrestling with the Bible.

WRITING STYLES

There are loads of different genres of movie: horror, documentary, chick-flick, western, sci-fi, mutant zombie octopus romantic comedy etc. A genre is a way of dividing stuff by its type or style rather than specific content or storyline. There are loads of different genres in the Bible — songs, prophecies, proverbs, laments, visions, speeches, parables, historical narrative. Identifying the genre of a Bible bit is important to how we understand it.

When David says in Psalm 22, *"I am poured out like water"*, he's not describing a miracle in which his whole body became liquid. It's poetry; we're not supposed to take it literally. On the other hand, when the Gospels record Jesus' tomb was empty, they mean it actually was physically empty. It is real history.

Sadly, we can't give you a guaranteed 100% accurate way of deciding the genre of a Bible passage. Occasionally it's controversial, such as with Genesis chapter 1, where there has been loads of heated debate on whether the creation in six days refers to a literal period of 6 x 24 hours, or whether it is a poetic way of speaking about the careful, ordered way in which God made the universe. However, most of the time, it's pretty obvious.

STUFF THAT REALLY HAPPENED

When we read in the Bible of things that actually occurred, it's easy to look for the spiritual lesson behind it and forget that it was a real, historical event. The crossing of the Red Sea in Exodus teaches us loads about God rescuing His people. But before we get to that teaching, we need to stop and think: *"Hang on, this actually happened! God parted the waters of the sea, and made water stand up like a wall. And the people walked through the middle on dry ground!"* An amazing miracle by God. And it really happened, it's not just a cool story. It is real history. How exciting is that!

STUFF NOT TO TAKE LITERALLY

There are other genres in the Bible which we shouldn't take literally. For example, parables. Jesus' parable of the sower (Mark 14 v 1–20) is not advice on farming — it's teaching us much bigger things. We're normally pretty good at switching into non-literal mode when we read parables or poems. Where we sometimes get it wrong is with the genre known as 'apocalyptic' that covers Revelation, Daniel and parts of Ezekiel and Zechariah. Those books are partly made up of visions and dreams with vivid and bizarre images. Some Christians take these passages very literally, but we think that's a mistake.

In Revelation 21 v 2, John sees the heavenly city *"coming down from heaven"*. When he looks again a few verses later, it is still *"coming down from heaven"* (21 v 10). And according to 3 v 12, this is what it always does. But surely it's got too reach its destination sooner or later. But that's not the point. The isn't a literal description of movement, but a poetical description description of what kind of city it is — a coming-down-from-heaven city! A city that is from God. The city itself (not the people who live there) is dressed like a bride (21 v 2). Skyscrapers wearing dresses sound ridiculous. Of course, that won't happen physically. It's symbolic of the fact that the city (representing all God's people) is destined for an intimate, permanent, loving relationship (like a marriage) with Jesus.

The visions in apocalyptic parts of the Bible are pictures and symbols that teach us truths about God and our relationship with Him. It's not always obvious what they are pictures of, but we must be careful not to take them too literally.

GIVE IT A GO

Try identifying the genre of the following Bible bits. Should you interpret them as historical or symbolic?

Judges 9 v 8–15
2 Samuel 12 v 1–6
1 Kings 17 v 8–16
Ezekiel 46 v 19–24 (look at ch. 47)
Matthew 5 v 29–30
Matthew 14 v 6–11
Exodus 9 v 22–24 and Revelation 16 v 21 (you might not get the same answer for both of them!)

Ideas taken from Dig Deeper by Nigel Beynon and Andrew Sach (available from Good Book Company website).

Jeremiah

Prophet in pain

Looking for a fun, exciting book with lots of action and people happily living God's way? Well, you're in the wrong place. Jeremiah's book is pretty miserable. God's people keep rejecting Him and God is far from happy. It's going to get messy. But there is plenty of action — powerful nations attacking each other.

The Old Testament tells us how God chose a people for Himself. They became the nation of Israel. God rescued them from slavery in Egypt, committed Himself to them, made them great promises and lived with them. But their relationship was a sticky one. God was totally faithful to them but they were completely faithless to Him.

After King Solomon, Israel split into a northern kingdom, Israel (capital: Samaria) and a southern one, Judah (capital: Jerusalem). Israel repeatedly disobeyed God and suffered His punishment when they were invaded in 722BC and totally trashed. Did Judah learn from that? Would they turn back to God? Well, it was to Judah that Jeremiah spoke God's message...

God had rescued His people and made a covenant with them — He promised to give them a great life if they obeyed His laws. It was the job of the prophets to call God's people back to the covenant. To remind them of the privileges and responsibilities of being God's special people.

Through Jeremiah, God told His people exactly what He thought of their behaviour. He warned them about the consequences, then unleashed His punishment. Jeremiah's book is no cuddly bedtime story. But if you want to discover exactly what God's like, hold your breath and read on.

49 | A call for Jeremiah

Ever heard people talk about being "called by God" to do something? Very few people have been chosen by God to serve Him in as dramatic a way as Jeremiah. Let's see how his bizarre story begins...

👁 **Read Jeremiah 1 v 1–10**

ENGAGE YOUR BRAIN

▷ *What's in Jeremiah's book? (v1–2)*

▷ *What does v5 tell us about God?*

▷ *What job does God give Jeremiah? (v5, v10)*

▷ *How does He answer Jeremiah's excuses? (v6–9)*

God's spokesman, Jeremiah, had to speak God's message at a time when the major superpowers (Assyria, Egypt, Babylon) were in violent conflict. Tiny Judah got caught in the middle. God gave Jeremiah a hugely tough and important job, and gave him the authority and strength to carry it out (v10).

👁 **Read verses 11–19**

▷ *What would happen to God's people? (v15)*

▷ *Why? (v16)*

▷ *How did God encourage Jeremiah to stick at it? (v17–19)*

Jeremiah, armed only with God's orders and promises, would deliver an unpleasant message of judgment — God would overthrow nations. A tough life lay ahead for Jeremiah. But God would be with him, protecting him and rescuing him in dark times, among terrifying enemies.

PRAY ABOUT IT

Thank God that He uses His people in amazing ways. Thank Him that He's always faithful and looks after His people, whatever they face.

THE BOTTOM LINE

God is with His people.
He rescues them.

→ **TAKE IT FURTHER**

Call waiting... on page 117.

50 Court in the act

Quiet. You're in a courtroom. And a trial's in progress. God is both prosecution lawer and judge. He speaks first. The accused is Israel, God's chosen people.

👁 Read Jeremiah 2 v 1–13

ENGAGE YOUR BRAIN

▷ *How had things started off for God's people? v2–3)*

▷ *But then how did they treat God?*

Back in Exodus, God rescued His people from Egypt, then made a covenant with them. A bit like a marriage. God promised to give them a great life if they obeyed His laws. But they refused to obey God and even worshipped false gods. Pathetic.

👁 Read verses 20–28

▷ *What do the pictures in v20–25 tell us about the Israelites?*

👁 Read verses 29-37

▷ *What did God's people claim? (v35)*

▷ *But what was the truth? (v32, v34)*

God's people rejected Him for a lifestyle that served their lust and involved idol worship. And they trashed His covenant in favour of begging help from nations who would only trick them. And then they had the arrogance to speak to God as if nothing had changed. God wanted His people to admit the charges. To plead guilty. Only then could repentance and forgiveness begin. More on this tomorrow.

PRAY ABOUT IT

Does anything in chapter 2 remind you of the way you treat God? Talk with Him about it. Be honest. And ask Him to help you change for the better.

→ TAKE IT FURTHER

More evidence on page 117.

51 | Return ticket

Jeremiah said rejecting God was like walking out on a marriage. It was cheating on God. That raises a big question: if God's people ever turned back, would He accept them?

Read Jeremiah 3 v 1–11

ENGAGE YOUR BRAIN

▷ How had the people been two-faced? (v4–5)

▷ Why were Judah's actions worse than Israel's (v6–8, v10)

God's people treated Him terribly. Judah saw Israel swept away in God's judgment, yet did just the same, refusing to remain faithful. Her superficial, short-lived change of heart was a waste of time too (v10).

Read 3 v 12 – 4 v 4

▷ What was God's great offer to His people? (v14–18)

▷ What must they do? (4 v 1–4)

Despite turning to other gods and constantly rejecting the Lord, He offered them a way back. God is so gracious and forgiving. He promises to pour out His blessings when His people do return to Him. And not just

people from Israel and Judah. Since Jesus died on the cross for all people, the offer is open to everyone.

THINK IT OVER

▷ What are the possible responses to God?

▷ And what's your response to God's amazing offer?

PRAY ABOUT IT

Say sorry to God for the times you choose other things above Him. Thank Him for His incredible mercy despite the way you've treated Him.

THE BOTTOM LINE

God offers to bring us back to Himself.

→ **TAKE IT FURTHER**

(Re)turn to page 117 for more.

52 Poetic justice

Today Jeremiah recites a poem. It's all about God's judgment against His people — no surprises there. But this is no ordinary poem. Jeremiah wants the readers to shake with fear as they read what God will do.

Read Jeremiah 4 v 5–18

ENGAGE YOUR BRAIN

- What will happen to God's people? (v6–9)

- What was the cause of this horrible situation? (v18)

- What was still a possibility? (v14)

Judah's time was up. God was sick of their selfish, sinful, disobedient ways and would punish them. They fully deserved it.

Read verses 19–31

- Why was Jeremiah upset? (v19–20)

- What remained God's verdict? (v22, v28)

- How did the people act, even while facing destruction? (v30)

Jeremiah described God's punishment of His people as reducing the world to a cosmic nothingness (v23–26), just as it was before God created everything. But there was a tiny shred of hope (v27).

And yet, in the face of such terrifying judgment, the people took no notice. They still rejected God, choosing other nations and their gods over Him (v30). Judah was like a prostitute (v30). Expecting to give birth, but about to be butchered to death (v31).

Do you think that's a disgusting picture? Well, it's how God felt about the way His people treated Him. Have you learned that about God yet? He hates sin and will punish it. Only Jesus can rescue us.

THINK IT OVER

- Do you take sin seriously enough?
- Will you run away from it and turn back to God?
- Or ignore it as these people did?

→ TAKE IT FURTHER

Is God's judgment too harsh? P117.

53 | Just one good man!

Today Jeremiah talks about happy times and fluffy kittens. OK, maybe not. It's not really his style, is it? He's still preaching about God's judgment, as the enemy armies gather on the horizon.

👁 Read Jeremiah 5 v 1–5

ENGAGE YOUR BRAIN

▷ *What was God's amazing offer? (v1)*

▷ *Could Jeremiah find one godly person? (v3–5)*

Do you still think God's punishment is too harsh? Look how willing He is to forgive! Yet these people said one thing and did another. Even their leaders refused to live God's way (v5).

👁 Read Jeremiah 6 v 16–30

▷ *What is still the invitation? (v16)*

▷ *How did the people answer? (v16–17)*

▷ *So what would happen to them?*

They refused to obey God and live for Him. They thought their pointless sacrifices and religious rituals would be enough (v20). Wrong.

Did you notice Jeremiah's role in all this (v27)? Like a metal inspector, testing God's people. And the conclusion (v30)? No purity to be found in Judah — they were like rejected silver and would be thrown away. God's judgment was on it's way. But the God who brings this punishment — what's He like?

PRAY ABOUT IT

Look back to see what these chapters actually tell us about God's character and capability. And take serious note. What will you say to Him now?

THE BOTTOM LINE

Because of Jesus, everyone has the chance to turn back to God, but many reject Him.

→ TAKE IT FURTHER

The bit we missed out is on page 118.

Don't read this page

If you're bothered by Jeremiah being so blunt... or upset when people refuse to listen... or squeamish about blood... or you think God's judgment is unfair... or you're happy keeping God at a distance... then don't read this next bit.

👁 Read Jeremiah 7 v 1–20

ENGAGE YOUR BRAIN

▷ What promise did God remind His people of? (v3)

▷ What changes would they have to make? (v4–6)

▷ What did they rely on instead of God? (v4, v18)

▷ What had God done again and again? (v13)

▷ How did the people respond?

▷ So what would happen? (v15)

These people went to God's temple and offered sacrifices to Him. But it was empty worship. They continued to sin horribly but thought their rituals and religion would save them. They were wrong. They refused to live God's way and He would throw them away (v15).

👁 Read Jeremiah 8 v 1–3

▷ What would happen to people who worshipped stars?

God's people hadn't given up on religion — far from it. But they followed man-made religion that had nothing to do with God.

GET ON WITH IT

God's people claimed His help while living incredibly immoral lives. They gave Him offerings, but their attention was elsewhere.

▷ Do you ever treat God that way?

▷ What sin do you need to cut out?

▷ How can you start obeying God more?

Talk these things over with the Lord.

→ TAKE IT FURTHER
Missing Jeremiah on page 118.

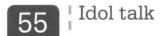

55 | Idol talk

Let's open Jeremiah's scrap book. It's full of pictures and snippets to remind God's people why punishment was on its way.

👁 Read Jeremiah 9 v 23–26

ENGAGE YOUR BRAIN

▶ What qualities can't rescue us from God's judgment? (v23)

▶ What can? (v24)

We can't rescue ourselves, however hard we try. Only God's kindness, justice and righteousness can. These were shown ultimately in Jesus dying to take the punishment for us.

👁 Read 10 v 1–16

▶ What did people worship instead of God? (v3–5)

▶ What did they forget about God? (v6–7, v12–13, v16)

👁 Read verses 23–25

▶ What did Jeremiah recognise about God?

THINK IT OVER

God's people swapped the living God for idols they could see and control.

Seems unbelievable, doesn't it?

▶ But how do we make the same mistake?

▶ What are you tempted to run after instead of God?

PRAY ABOUT IT

Ask God to help you put Him first, and to get rid of anything in your life that takes His place.

THE BOTTOM LINE

Nothing and no one is more powerful, terrifying and loving than God — worship Him. Nothing else.

→ TAKE IT FURTHER

Idly stride along to page 118.

Slaughter them, God!

Do you complain much? Some people seem to actually enjoy moaning when life is hard. It can help to get things off your chest. But do you ever complain to God? Jeremiah did. Loads.

👁 Read Jeremiah 11v18–12v6

ENGAGE YOUR BRAIN

▶ How did Jeremiah know about the plot to kill him? (v18)

▶ What did they have planned for Jeremiah? (v19, v21)

▶ How did God deal with them? (v22–23)

▶ Was Jeremiah happy with that? (v1–4)

▶ What was God saying to Jeremiah? (v5–6)

Jeremiah was right in wanting sin against God to be punished. But he seemed to be wanting revenge. God's reply was: Leave that to me — you've got your own troubles to deal with. Believe it or not, life would get even tougher for Jeremiah.

Believers aren't promised an easy life. In fact, we're told we will have to suffer in this life, just as Jesus suffered for us. But one day, when Jesus returns, our suffering will end forever.

👁 Read verses 7–17

▶ Do you think it was easy for God to punish His own people?

▶ What hope was there in the middle of judgment? (v15–16)

God won't let sin go unpunished. But there is still hope. He longs for people to come back to Him and learn to live His way.

PRAY ABOUT IT

Pray about injustice in the world. Think of specific stories of Christians being persecuted. Ask God for justice to be done. And ask Him to help you to not take revenge when you feel wrongly treated. Thank God that He's the completely fair Judge.

→ TAKE IT FURTHER

Judge for yourself on page 118.

57 | Belt up!

Imagine owning a great, shiny belt that you really like. Now imagine going rock-climbing, taking off your belt and leaving it hidden in the rocks until it rotted. Well, that's what God told Jeremiah to do.

👁 Read Jeremiah 13 v 1–11

ENGAGE YOUR BRAIN

▶ *What was the belt a picture of?*

▶ *What had God's people done instead of serving Him? (v10)*

Poor old Jeremiah. Trekking all that way, knowing his belt would be ruined when he got there. But that's the point. If Judah (or you or I) choose to walk stubbornly in the wrong direction, we know what the results will be. We will be as useless as that rotting belt. Only fit to be thrown away.

👁 Read verses 12–14

What's this about the people of Judah being drunk? It's another picture to make a point. They will drink from the *cup of God's wrath* — they will be fully punished by Him. It's another way of saying they're about to experience the devastating power and anger of God.

👁 Read verses 15–17

▶ *What must people do before it's too late? (v16)*

▶ *Why don't they listen to God? (v15, v17)*

Pride and arrogance often get in the way of people listening to God and giving Him the glory He deserves. They want to take control of their own lives and refuse to let God take charge. Pride can stop us from living God's way.

PRAY ABOUT IT

Pray for people you know (maybe yourself?) who are too proud to let God be King of their lives. Ask Him to break through their arrogance so they realise their need to turn to Jesus.

THE BOTTOM LINE

People proudly living their own way are like useless, rotting rags to God.

→ TAKE IT FURTHER

Page 118 — it's a belter!

58 | God's deadline

Today's big question: Is there ever a time when God won't forgive us? Did you answer "No"? If so, you're in for a big shock.

👁 Read Jeremiah 14 v 1–12

ENGAGE YOUR BRAIN

▷ What was the big problem in Judah? (v1)

▷ What did Jeremiah ask God? (v7)

▷ What was God's devastating reply? (v12)

God's people accused Him of wandering off (v8), but it was they who had run away from God (v10). There comes a time when God's patience with those who disobey Him runs out. If you keep rejecting God, one day it will be too late to ask Him to rescue you.

👁 Read Jeremiah 15 v 10–21

▷ What was Jeremiah's first complaint? (v10)

▷ How did God answer him? (v11)

▷ What else was bothering the prophet? (v18)

▷ Why was it getting him down so much? (v15–17)

▷ What did God tell him to do? (v19)

▷ And what did God say He would do? (v20–21)

Jeremiah had hit rock bottom. Delivering God's final judgment made everyone hate him. But God called him back to his task with a boost (v20–21). If anyone had failed it was Jeremiah, not God. But the Lord was with Him. Always. God promised to rescue him.

PRAY ABOUT IT

Have you hit rock bottom? Are you fed up of it all? Then pour everything out to God. Tell Him exactly how you feel. God is faithful and is always with you. Only He can rescue you and protect you.

→ TAKE IT FURTHER
Missing bits on page 119.

59 | Who do you trust?

Who do you trust? Whose hands would you put your life in? Is there anyone? God asks the same question to the people of Judah. And to us. Who do you trust?

👁 **Read Jeremiah 17 v 1–4**

ENGAGE YOUR BRAIN

▶ *Can you work out what their sin was? (v2)*

▶ *What was God's response? (v3–4)*

The guilt of God's people was *engraved* on their hearts — it was permanent. They had turned to fake gods (like Asherah) and had smashed God's covenant with them. God's anger, once stirred, wouldn't be easily removed (v4).

👁 **Read verses 5–10**

▶ *What happens when people choose themselves over trusting in God? (v5–6)*

▶ *What about those who trust in the Lord? (v7–8)*

▶ *What does God look at, ultimately? (v10)*

Put your trust in the world's idea of success and happiness and guess what happens. You may be happy for a while, but in the end, God sees your heart and He'll give you what you deserve. If you've put your trust in Him then you've nothing to fear (v8). But if your heart is in the wrong place, then you'll be punished along with Judah.

THINK IT OVER
Be ruthlessly honest with yourself. Have you put your trust in God and in the death of His Son in your place? Or have you decided to go your own way? It's not a decision you can put off — you don't know when it will become too late to change.

PRAY ABOUT IT
Do you need to thank God, confess to Him or turn to Him? Or all three?

THE BOTTOM LINE
Who will you put your trust in?

→ **TAKE IT FURTHER**
Loads more on page 119.

PSALMS: Stewing in silence

Time for a few psalms. Let's start with a tricky one. David is thinking about some serious issues, including illness, death, sin and God's discipline. But there's hope too...

👁 **Read all of Psalm 39**

ENGAGE YOUR BRAIN

▷ *What sort of mood does David seem to be in?*

👁 **Read verses 1–3**

▷ *What has David decided to do? (v1)*

▷ *Why has he made this particular decision?*

▷ *Why did he change his mind?*

David doesn't want to make his situation worse than it already is. Yet he struggles to keep silent. He is frustrated and angry. Let's see how he works out his emotions towards God and this situation.

👁 **Read verses 4–6**

▷ *What is David seeking? (v4)*

▷ *How does he express humility?*

👁 **Read verses 7–13**

▷ *What is David asking? (v8, v10)*

▷ *What confidence does he show in the Lord?*

▷ *What is David's final desire?*

No matter how difficult things get, David's hope remains in God (v7). He sees that his sin caused the hard times he is facing, and that ultimately God is using this experience to make David humbly dependent on Him.

▷ *How do you react to God's discipline?*

▷ *In what areas do you find it hard to obey Him?*

PRAY ABOUT IT

This psalm gives us an example of confessing sin and seeking help and comfort. Use David's words as an example as you pray today.

→ **TAKE IT FURTHER**

Turn in silence to page 119.

61 | Mood music

Do you have moodswings? One moment you're bouncing with happiness, the next you're fuming angrily, the next you're quiet and sad. David had moodswings. Follow his feelings in this psalm.

👁 **Read Psalm 40 v 1–5**

ENGAGE YOUR BRAIN

▷ What was David's past experience of God? (v1–2)

▷ What had David learned? (v4)

▷ How many great things had God done? (v5)

▷ What can you thank and praise God for?

👁 **Read verses 6–10**

▷ What did David want to do? (v8)

▷ How did he do it? (v9–10)

What's this about God piercing David's ears (v6)??? Back then, piercing your ears for someone was saying: I'll be your servant for life. David belonged to God and he showed it in his willingness to talk to other people about God.

SHARE IT

▷ Do you belong to God?

▷ How will you show it in what you talk about?

👁 **Read verses 11–17**

▷ Why did David need God's help? (v12)

▷ What does David want? (v14–15)

▷ What else? (v16)

Verses 16–17 show us David's different moods — his praise to God, his reliance on God, his cry for help.

PRAY ABOUT IT

Spend time with God, thanking Him for specific things; committing yourself to serving Him; asking Him to help you with anything that's weighing on your mind.

→ **TAKE IT FURTHER**

Stay in the mood on page 119.

62 | Highs and lows

As with the last two psalms, David is ill, feeling low and needs God's help. Can you sympathise with that feeling? Ever feel like that? Check out how David copes with this hopeless situation.

👁 Read all of Psalm 41

David said his illness was due to God punishing his sin. Even worse, David's enemies were loving it and were spreading lies about him. And even worse than that, his best pal turned against him. And that's what really hurt. But David found confidence in God.

👁 Read verses 1–3

ENGAGE YOUR BRAIN

▶ *What attitude does God like to see? (v1)*
▶ *How does God treat His people similarly? (v2–3)*
▶ *Who do you need to look out for and care for?*
▶ *How will you do that?*

The rest of the Bible reminds us that one day all pain and suffering will be gone — in God's new heavens and earth.

👁 Read verses 4–13

▶ *What did David's enemies do?*

▶ *But what really hurt him? (v9)*
▶ *What was David sure of about God? (v12)*

David was ill and in need, but there were no verse-1-type people to look after him. Instead, his enemies were gloating and spreading lies about him. Even his close friend let him down. *"Lifted up his heel"* is like saying: *He kicked me when I was down.* But David knew he could always rely on God. He's the God who brings sinners into a permanent, close relationship with Himself (v12). Superb.

PRAY ABOUT IT

Verse 13 rounds off the first book of psalms — all 41 of them. Why is the Lord worth praising? What would your reason be? Why not tell Him right now?

→ TAKE IT FURTHER

Lift your heel... and walk to page 120.

63 | Heart ache

Ever argue with yourself? Your head tells you one thing, but your heart tells you something else. In this psalm, the writer's head tells him to trust in the Lord, but in his heart he feels far from God.

👁 Read Psalm 42 v 1–4

ENGAGE YOUR BRAIN

▷ *How would you describe the writer's feelings, verse by verse?*
v1:
v2:
v3:
v4:

▷ *What did his enemies say? (v3)*

He was surrounded by his enemies, and he was understandably feeling down. He was far from from Jerusalem and its temple — the symbol of God's presence among His people — so he felt distant from God.

👁 Read verses 5–11

▷ *How does the writer feel, deep down? (v6–7, v9–10)*

▷ *But what does he remember about God? (v8)*

▷ *What does his head keep telling his heart? (v5, v11)*

The psalm writer was feeling far from God. And yet he never stopped talking to the Lord. He was brutally honest with God about how he was feeling. And he still longed to be close to God.

PRAY ABOUT IT

Tell God exactly how you're feeling right now — whether you're on a high, down in the depths, or somewhere in between. Ask Him to help you thirst for Him — so that you long to know Him better and love talking to Him.

→ TAKE IT FURTHER

Follow your heart... to page 120.

Prisoner's progress

John Bunyan wrote one of the best-selling, most popular books of all time — *The Pilgrim's Progress*. But his life was far from easy, and he went through many struggles before he wrote this Christian classic.

TOUGH BEGINNINGS

John Bunyan was born in 1628 in the little village of Elstow, in Bedfordshire, England. His family were poor and, at the age of sixteen, John lost his mother and two sisters, who all died within months of each other. Soon afterwards, John left home and joined the army, having fallen out with his father.

After fighting in the English Civil War, Bunyan left the army and married Mary. She had hardly any possessions, apart from two Christian books. With these, Mary taught John to read and the books had a huge impact on him. The next four years were a time of intense spiritual struggle. His journey to becoming a Christian is very similar to that of the main character in *The Pilgrim's Progress* — facing such enemies as humiliation, doubt and despair. John knew that he was a sinner and feared God's anger against him. One evening he was playing

a game and, in his own words: *"A voice did suddenly dart from heaven into my soul which said, 'Wilt thou leave thy sins and go to heaven, or have thy sins and go to hell?'"*

LONG ROAD TO FORGIVENESS

John started going to church and had many conversations about Christianity with the pastor, John Gifford. He also started to read the Bible more, but he still struggled with feelings of depression and doubt about his faith. Surely God couldn't forgive someone as sinful as him! For several years he continued to struggle with such thoughts until one day, when he was working in a field, he heard the words: *"Thy righteousness is in heaven"*. As Bunyan put it himself: *"I saw with the eyes of my soul Jesus Christ at God's right hand — there, I say, is my righteousness, today and forever."* He trusted in Jesus' death in his place — he now realised his sins were forgiven.

PUNISHED FOR PREACHING

In 1660, King Charles II came to power and declared that people were only allowed to worship in their local Anglican church, and nowhere else. However, Bunyan continued to preach anywhere and everywhere without a license from the king. He was arrested and sentenced to three months in Bedford Jail, yet he was kept in prison for 12 years!

John could have been released at any time, but only on the condition that he stopped preaching. Of course, he refused. Imprisonment and persecution didn't damage John's faith at all. He regularly preached to groups of prisoners and it was in prison that he wrote many of his books, including *The Pilgrim's Progress*. Eventually, Bunyan was released from jail in 1672 and was allowed to preach again, which he did with great enthusiasm, to large crowds.

PILGRIM'S PROGRESS

Not that life was ever easy. In 1675, the preaching licenses of many 'Nonconformists' were withdrawn and John was again imprisoned for six months. In 1678, *The Pilgrim's Progress* was finally published. It was instantly popular and has remained so ever since, having had a huge impact on millions of readers worldwide. It's an allegory (word picture) of a man's journey to becoming a Christian. The main character, Christian, travels from his home in the City of Destruction to Celestial City (heaven). On the way, he passes through many bizarre places — such as the Slough of Despond, the village of Morality, Doubting Castle, and the Hill of Difficulty — and meets such colourful characters as Evangelist, the giant Despair and Mr Worldly Wisemanl. It's packed full of characters and situations recognisable to everyone. Why not check out Pilgrim's Progress for yourself and see if you can identify with Christian's journey to the heavenly city?

The Pilgrim's Progress by John Bunyan can be found in most bookshops and on book websites.

64 | LUKE: Walking with Jesus

Back on the road with Jesus. Despite the opposition to Jesus, there's still a large crowd travelling with Him. It's time for Jesus to give them (and us) a reality check...

👁 Read Luke 14 v 25–35

ENGAGE YOUR BRAIN

▷ *Compared to how they feel about Jesus, how must his followers feel about their families and themselves? (v26)*

▷ *What do real disciples do? (v27)*

▷ *What does that mean?*

Jesus isn't saying hate your relatives. He's saying you can't follow Him half-heartedly. Either He's your number one, and you're willing to suffer for Him, or you're not. Either you're a 100% follower, or you're no follower.

▷ *If you want to build a tower, what do you do before starting? (v28)*

▷ *Otherwise, what'll happen? (v29–30)*

▷ *What's Jesus encouraging people to do before they start following Him?*

Following Jesus is like running a marathon; it's the finishing that counts, not the starting. Before you start, you must decide to keep going to the finish even when it hurts. Same with following Christ! Still, it's better to be on Jesus' side than opposing Him, like it's better for a king to be at peace with a stronger king instead of getting slaughtered by him (v31–32).

THINK IT THROUGH

▷ *If you're considering becoming a Christian... what's Jesus telling you to do first? (v28–30)*

▷ *If you're already a Christian... what's Jesus telling you following Him will be like? (v27)*

PRAY ABOUT IT

I'm guessing you've got loads to talk to God about today.

→ TAKE IT FURTHER

Keep walking... to page 120.

65 | Get ready to party

Everyone likes a good party. Birthdays, end of exams, weddings, or just because you fancy it. But when does heaven have a party?

👁 Read Luke 15 v 1–2

ENGAGE YOUR BRAIN

▶ *What type of people want to listen to Jesus? (v1)*

▶ *How do the Pharisees feel about that? (v2)*

So Jesus tells these religious leaders a couple of stories to make a point…

👁 Read v 3–10

and draw what happens in them.

▶ *What prompts heaven to throw a party? (v7, v10)*

GET ON WITH IT

▶ *What do these two parables tell us was Jesus' priority for His time on earth?*

▶ *If you're a follower of Jesus, what should your priority be?*

▶ *What should you most rejoice about in life?*

PRAY ABOUT IT

Think of a couple of people you know who are "lost". Pray for opportunities to tell them about how Jesus offers them eternal life, and pray that Jesus would find them so that you and everyone in heaven can celebrate.

THE BOTTOM LINE

Jesus' priority is to find and rescue sinners; and heaven has a party when sinners turn to God.

➔ TAKE IT FURTHER

Party on, dude. Page 120.

66 | Two ways to get it wrong

Jesus is in story-telling mode – here's another famous parable. Get this, and you get Jesus' mission, so we'll spend two sessions on it.

☉ Read Luke 15 v11–32

ENGAGE YOUR BRAIN

▷ What does the younger son say and do? (v12–13)

▷ Where does living this way get him? (v14–16)

By v16, the younger son's outside his father's house and his life is ruined! So he decides to go back (we'll get to that next time). But now let's meet the older brother…

▷ When his father welcomes the younger son back into his house, how does the older brother react? (v28)

▷ He's been "slaving" for his father — what was he hoping his dad would give him? (v29)

The older son didn't seem to be working hard out of love for his father — he was in it for the reward. And he ends the story outside his father's house, refusing to go in.

The first son ignored his father and took his gifts; the second son was being good so he could earn rewards from his father. Jesus is saying everyone's like that with God; you're either a "sinner" (v1), who has taken God's good gifts and ignored Him, or you're a "Pharisee" (v2), who only obeys God's rules to try to earn eternal life. Neither of these attitudes loves God; neither brings us to God's house — eternal life in His kingdom.

PRAY ABOUT IT
Pray for people you know who are like either of the brothers. Pray that they will understand the only way to eternal life — through Jesus Christ.

THE BOTTOM LINE
Ignoring God completely and trying to be good enough both leave us outside God's kingdom.

→ TAKE IT FURTHER
No Take It Further today.

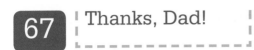

67 | Thanks, Dad!

The younger son took his father's gifts, ignored his father, and ruined his life. But then he came to his senses...

👁 **Read Luke 15 v11–32**

ENGAGE YOUR BRAIN

▷ *The son was hoping he could work for his father (v18) — but when the father saw him, what did he say? (v22–24)*

From starving in a pigsty to a massive party in his father's house — the son's life is so much better with his father than on his own.

▷ *What did the father do when he saw his son in the distance?*

For a man in that society, this would have involved total humiliation. To meet the son and welcome him home, this father had to leave his house and shame himself.

👁 **Turn to 2 Corinthians 8 v 9**

▷ *What did Jesus do to welcome people into the riches of heaven?*

God left heaven, became a man, and was humiliated in death – just

to meet us and welcome us to His heavenly party. Incredible.

PRAY ABOUT IT

While the younger son enjoyed the party, the older son finished the story outside, refusing to go in (v 28).

▷ *Which son are you?*

▷ *Do you need to thank God for welcoming you in so you can enjoy life with Him?*

▷ *Or do you need to ask God to welcome you in today so you can begin life with Him?*

THE BOTTOM LINE

Life's indescribably better with God than on our own; and God welcomes us into eternal life even though we don't deserve it.

➡ **TAKE IT FURTHER**

Feast your eyes on page 120.

68 Money money money

This is one of Jesus' stranger parables — but basically it's all about how we use money.

👁 Read Luke 16 v 1–9

ENGAGE YOUR BRAIN

▶ *The manager had influence and wealth — what did he use it to do? (v4)*

He's sensible — he wants people to still welcome him when he no longer has a job.

▶ *What does Jesus tell His followers to do with their worldly wealth? (v9)*

▶ *Why? (end of v 9)*

Jesus isn't saying it's OK to cheat. The point He's making is this: use whatever you've got now to serve God — and you'll find a bunch of friends who last beyond death. Wouldn't it be great if you gave money to a missionary organisation and someone you'd never met welcomed you into eternity, because your money had enabled someone to tell him about Jesus?

👁 Read verses 10–15

Notice v13 — we're to devote our money to God, not devote ourselves to money as our god.

GET ON WITH IT

▶ *Are you mainly using your worldly wealth for yourself, to have friends now, or for God, so you're welcomed in eternal life?*

▶ *How can you use your money and possessions to serve God?*

PRAY ABOUT IT

Ask God to show you how you could usefully use what He's given you.

→ TAKE IT FURTHER

Verses 16–18 are on page 121.

69 | A serious warning

You're about to be hit by a car when someone shouts: "Get out of the way!" They're doing that to help you, not shock you — and that's why Jesus talks about hell...

👁 **Read Luke 16 v 19–26**

ENGAGE YOUR BRAIN

▷ *In the parable, what happens to the rich man? (v22–23)*

▷ *How is hell described? (v23–24)*

▷ *What else does Jesus reveal about hell? (v26)*

Jesus is warning people not to ignore God and end up in hell. But hang on, what gives Jesus the right to tell people about hell?

👁 **Read verses 27–31**

▷ *What does the rich man want to happen, and why?*

▷ *But they haven't listened to Old Testament teaching — would anything convince them? (v31)*

Jesus has authority to warn us about hell because He's the One who would rise from the dead. He's warning us, not to shock us but to help us.

He wants us to listen to God's word, to repent (turn back to God and ask for forgiveness), and to enjoy eternal life with Him, rather than ignoring Him and experiencing hell.

PRAY ABOUT IT

▷ *Do you need to repent and ask God to forgive you?*
▷ *Do you need to ask God to give you opportunities to tell your family and friends about heaven and hell?*

THE BOTTOM LINE
The risen Jesus has the authority to tell us about hell — and He says it's real, painful, and final.

⤵ **TAKE IT FURTHER**
More fiery talk on page 121.

70 Your problem, my problem

"No man is an island", a poet once wrote. We live among other people and our lives affect theirs. How much do you care about Christians you know who are sinning? What do you do about it?

Read verses 1–4

ENGAGE YOUR BRAIN

▷ Who does Jesus say "woe", or trouble, will come to? (v1)

▷ How serious is He? (v2)

Lesson 1 — We must not cause others to sin

▷ If a Christian we know sins, what should we do? (middle of v3)

▷ Why is this so amazingly hard?

Lesson 2 — We must rebuke Christians when they sin

That doesn't mean shouting at people. It means gently but firmly telling someone that what they've done is wrong.

▷ If a Christian repents (accepts they were wrong and turns back to God), what should we do, even if they've hurt us? (v3–4)

▷ Why is this so hard?

Lesson 3 – We must forgive Christians when they repent

Jesus isn't asking us to do anything He didn't do. He never caused others to sin; He always gently rebuked those who were sinning; He forgave His followers when they repented.

GET ON WITH IT

▷ How do your words or actions encourage others to sin?

▷ Is there anyone you need to help face up to their sin?

▷ Or anyone you need to forgive?

PRAY ABOUT IT

Pray you'll help your Christian friends in these three ways.

→ TAKE IT FURTHER

More top tips on page 121.

71 Who's on whose side?

**Should God be thankful we're on His side?
Or should we be grateful He's on ours?
Or is it both?**

👁 Read Luke 17 v 5–6

ENGAGE YOUR BRAIN

▶ *What can even a small amount of faith in God achieve?*

Jesus is telling us something really important about faith here. The power of faith doesn't come from its owner (you) but from its object — who you've got faith in. A lot of faith in your school soccer team to win the World Cup is no use — the faith is in the wrong team. A small amount of faith in the Creator God to do whatever He likes is massively powerful. So if a Christian does something great, it's not them doing something great because they have lots of faith; it's God doing something great because God is amazingly powerful.

👁 Read v 7–10

▶ *If a servant just does what it's his job to do, does he deserve thanks? (v9)*

▶ *When a servant of God has done what He asks, do we deserve loads of thanks? (v10)*

Christians are privileged to be God's servants. When we do things for Him, it's only what He deserves — we have no right to think that He owes us.

PRAY ABOUT IT

Thank you for…

Please help me to remember…

THE BOTTOM LINE

When we do great things, it's actually God doing them through us; when we work for God, it's only what God deserves.

→ TAKE IT FURTHER

More stuff on page 121.

87

72 | Thanks, God!

My god-daughter is three, and she's just learned to say "Thank you" when someone does something for her. She could teach these guys a thing or two!

👁 Read Luke 17 v 11–14

ENGAGE YOUR BRAIN

▷ Who does Jesus meet, and what do they want? (v11–13)

Lepers were considered unclean, and so had to be cut off from God's people, the Jews.

▷ Jesus heals them in v13–14. How should they respond?

👁 Read v 15–19

▷ How many of them do say thank you? (v15–16)

▷ What else do we learn about the thankful leper in v16?

Nine of the lepers don't return to thank Jesus. Only one shows true faith. This was another example of God's people ignoring Jesus' message. So Jesus would take His message and healing to other nations, as shown by this Samaritan leper.

▷ How did this guy respond to being cured? (v15, v18)

▷ What does Jesus tell him has made him well? (v19)

This guy leaves not just with his leprosy cured, but with his heart cured. He leaves as a friend of God. True faith is seen in people thanking and praising God for saving them.

PRAY ABOUT IT

Has God cured your sin disease? Do you praise and thank Him? Will you do so right now?

THE BOTTOM LINE

Don't take Jesus saving you for granted; thank Him for it.

→ TAKE IT FURTHER

Challenging stuff on page 121.

73 Jesus: the return

Young kids and long car journeys are a bad mix. "Are we nearly there yet?" they constantly yell. Jesus has already said He'll return to the world. But the Pharisees want to know when. Are we nearly there yet?

👁 Read Luke 17 v 20–25

ENGAGE YOUR BRAIN

▷ What will Jesus' return be like? (v24)

▷ Will everyone know it's happening?

▷ But what must happen first? (v25)

👁 Read v26–30

▷ In Noah's time, how much warning was there that God was sending a flood? (1 Peter 3 v 20)

▷ So, what do we know it will be like when Jesus, the Son of Man, returns? (v26)

👁 Read v 31–37

Jesus' return will divide people — some will be left to live in His perfect kingdom: others will be shut out (v34–35).

▷ When Jesus returns, what shouldn't Christians do? (v31)

When Jesus returns, Christians will live in His perfect world. So we should be looking forward to His return more than anything else! More than holidays, or falling in love, or getting our dream job, or making money — more than anything! If we're not looking forward to it, we haven't understood how great it'll be for Christians when Jesus returns. If we understand that, then we'll realise that v33 is true!

GET ON WITH IT

How do you need to change your thinking and attitudes, based on Jesus' words here?

PRAY ABOUT IT

Lord Jesus, Thank you that you will return. Help me to be ready for that day by trusting in you; help me to look forward to that day more than anything else.

→ TAKE IT FURTHER

More about Jesus' return on p122.

74 | Do something, God!

There's so much wrong in this world, so much God doesn't like. Should we just ignore it? Is there anything we can do? Why doesn't God seem to do much about it?

👁 Read Luke 18 v 1–5

ENGAGE YOUR BRAIN
▶ What's Jesus saying in this parable?

👁 Read verses 6–8
▶ If even this unjust judge was willing to give justice, what will the perfect God definitely do for His people? (v7–8)

▶ So, can we ask for justice confidently?

▶ When will we ultimately see this happen? (end of v8)

▶ So, will we always see God's justice immediately?

Verse 8 is confusing. Will God's justice come quickly or will we have to wait? Well, God answers our prayers quickly. Sometimes the answer may be "No" or "Wait", but He does answer. His ultimate and final justice will come when Jesus returns.

Around the world today, God's people will be unfairly treated because they're Christians. Some (maybe you) will be laughed at; others will be tortured; some will die. God will bring justice for His persecuted people when His Son Jesus returns. So we can pray confidently, we must pray patiently, we should pray persistently.

PRAY ABOUT IT
Why not visit www.opendoorsuk.org Pray for a particular group of persecuted Christians — that God would bring His justice for them. And thank Him that He will bring perfect justice when Jesus returns.

THE BOTTOM LINE
Jesus will return and bring God's justice — so pray for it and don't give up praying for it!

→ TAKE IT FURTHER
Do something — go to page 122.

75 Compare and contrast

Who do you compare yourself to? Are you a good person? A clever person? A successful person? Is there anyone you're glad you're not like? Anyone you look down on?

👁 Read Luke 18 v 9–12

ENGAGE YOUR BRAIN

▶ *Who went to the temple to pray?*
▶ *Who does the Pharisee compare himself to? (v11–12)*
▶ *Why does he think he's better than them?*

Here's a very good, very religious man. Compared to others he's great, and he knows it! And he clearly thinks that his goodness makes him right with God.

👁 Read v 13–14

▶ *How does the tax collector describe himself? (v13)*

He doesn't compare himself to others: he compares himself to God. He knows he's not good — he's a sinner.

▶ *So what does he ask God for?*

So, we've got a Pharisee who compares himself to others and is really good… and a tax collector who thinks he's not good because he compares himself to God.

▶ *Which of these guys goes home "justified" — put right with God?*

GET ON WITH IT

▶ *Who should we compare ourselves with — others, or God?*
▶ *What does comparing ourselves with God show us about ourselves? (think back to v13)*

PRAY ABOUT IT

▶ *Write your own prayer based on today's Bible bit.*

THE BOTTOM LINE

Compare yourself with God instead of others, and you'll see that the only way into His kingdom is to ask Him for mercy, not by trying to be good enough.

→ TAKE IT FURTHER

Verses 15–17 are covered on page 123.

76 | All you need

**Time for a big big question.
How can we have a good life now
and eternal life in the future?**

👁 Read Luke 18 v 18–30

ENGAGE YOUR BRAIN

▶ It's a great question in v18 —
how does Jesus answer in v19?

Here's a reminder of what we saw
yesterday — only God is totally,
utterly, perfectly, good.

▶ How does Jesus answer in v20?

And so to do enough to inherit
eternal life, you need to keep every
single one of God's commandments.

▶ How well is this guy doing? (v21)

What a claim! But Jesus knows the
man's heart and so challenges him to
give up his wealth and get on with
following Him (v22).

▶ How does this guy react? (v23)

It's impossible for anyone to live a life
good enough for God. No one can
earn eternal life.

▶ But what's the great news? (v27)

▶ Who does God give eternal life
to? (v28–30)

Did you notice in v30 it's not just after
we die that Jesus' followers receive a
better life — it's *"in this age"* as well!

GET ON WITH IT

▶ What kind of things do people
say you need to have a good life?

▶ What kind of things is it easy to
think you need to do to deserve
eternal life?

Remember, all you need to do is trust
in Jesus. Nothing else! Being good
and being rich doesn't bring full life,
now or in eternity — only following
Jesus does.

→ TAKE IT FURTHER

Get your teeth into page 122.

77 | Blind faith

We've been following Jesus through Luke's Gospel for a while now. Everything we've seen so far is now drawn together in one episode. So listen very carefully...

👁 Read Luke 18 v 31–34

ENGAGE YOUR BRAIN

Jesus reminds His followers He's going to Jerusalem. There He'll be rejected, die, and rise back to life (v32–33). The disciples don't get it (v34), but someone shows them what it's all about...

👁 Read v 35–43

Ⓓ *What does he call Jesus? (v38–39)*

David had been God's people's king. God promised that one of David's descendants would be God's promised, eternal King, His Christ. This blind guy can see who Jesus is!

Ⓓ *What does he want? (v38, v41)*

Ⓓ *Why does Jesus heal him? (v42)*

Ⓓ *What two responses does he make? (v43)*

Remember, Jesus is on the way to rejection and death. Following Him won't be easy — but he happily follows Jesus, the Son of David, who has healed him and saved him.

GET ON WITH IT

Ⓓ *Do you need for the first time to ask Jesus to heal you, to give you eternal life?*

Ⓓ *Do you need to get on with following Jesus and praising God even when that brings difficulty and rejection?*

PRAY ABOUT IT

Turn your answers into a prayer.

THE BOTTOM LINE

This blind beggar shows what Christianity's about: recognising Jesus, being saved through faith, and following Him even though it's hard.

→ TAKE IT FURTHER

Son shine on page 123.

78 | JEREMIAH: Prophet in pain

Let's get back to Jeremiah and his happy fluffy message. Oh, hold on, I'm thinking of someone else. As we rejoin the action, God's people are still rebelling against Him and Jeremiah is still telling them about God's judgment.

👁 Read Jeremiah 18 v 1–12

ENGAGE YOUR BRAIN

▷ What was happening to the pot? (v4)

▷ *Who is the potter and who are the pots? (v5–6)*

Even now, there's still time for God's disobedient people to change — to be re-formed by God into something better. But they refuse to change their stubborn, sinful ways (v12). God doesn't think much of that attitude...

👁 Read verses 13–17

▷ *What did they choose instead of living God's way? (v15)*

▷ *So what would be the result? (v16–17)*

God gave them chance after chance to turn back to Him. He warned them of the terrifying consequences if they refused. But they still wouldn't change. Sickening.

👁 Read Jeremiah 19 v 1–13

▷ *Why did Jeremiah smash the pot? (v10–12)*

God's people had turned their backs on Him and worshipped false gods instead (v4). God continuously warned them to turn back to Him or be punished. They refused again and again. So they would be smashed, just like the pot.

PRAY ABOUT IT

God, the Potter, would re-form His people — if only they turned back to Him. Do you need to do that? Know anyone who does? Talk to God about it.

THE BOTTOM LINE

Those who reject God will be smashed.

➡ TAKE IT FURTHER

Take a pot shot on page 123.

79 | Stocks and shares

Have you seen movies or TV set in medieval times, where criminals get beaten up, tortured and put in stocks? Well, it's another miserable day for Jeremiah, and guess what happens to him...

👁 Read Jeremiah 20 v 1–6

ENGAGE YOUR BRAIN
▷ What lesson would God's people get from the example of Pashur?

Head of temple security, Pashur, should have known better than terrorising God's prophet. God gave Pashur a new name which means *"terror on every side"* — and that's exactly what he would experience. Why? Because he went against God's messenger and pretended to be a prophet himself. Serious stuff.

👁 Read verses 7–13

▷ What happened to Jeremiah when he preached God's message? (v7–8)

▷ But could he keep God's words to himself? (v9)

▷ What did Jeremiah remember that gave him comfort? (v11)

▷ So what did he conclude? (v13)

👁 Read verses 14–18
▷ How did Jeremiah's mood suddenly change?

THINK IT OVER
How could he plunge so fast from trust in God to despairing self-pity?
▷ Never done the same?

▷ What firm truths will you learn to hold on to when life seems unbearable?

PRAY ABOUT IT
Thank God that He's with you even when life seems too much to bear. Tell Him what's getting you down. And praise Him for the great truths you know about Him.

THE BOTTOM LINE
Life is hard, but God is good.

→ TAKE IT FURTHER
God vs evil kings on page 123.

80 Back to the future

Has Jeremiah been getting you down? Lots of doom and gloom and judgment. Well, I hope you're sitting down because I have something shocking to say: Today, Jeremiah gives us GOOD NEWS! Honestly.

👁 Read Jeremiah 23 v 1–4

ENGAGE YOUR BRAIN

▷ *What had the leaders ("shepherds") of God's people been doing? (v1–2)*

▷ *So what would God do? (v2)*

▷ *What's the great news for God's people in the future? (v3–4)*

There was no hope of God removing His judgment. But there was hope of a future *after* God's judgment. He would rescue them again and give them a perfect King to rule them. The New Testament tells us this King is Jesus.

👁 Read verses 5–8

▷ *How will King Jesus rule His people? (v5)*

▷ *What will He be called? (v6)*

▷ *What will happen to God's chosen people? (v6, v8)*

King Zedekiah was a joke. A bad joke. He was a weak and pathetic figure who had only his own interests in mind. Ironically, Zedekiah's name means *"righteousness of the Lord"*! Which explains why God's perfect King is referred to by that name. God wasn't content with such a joke of a king — He had plans for a branch shooting out of David's dying dynasty who really would rule righteously — King Jesus.

PRAY ABOUT IT

Read verses 1–8 again, thanking God for His promises to His people. Use verses 5–6 to thank and praise Him for sending His rescuing Son, King Jesus.

THE BOTTOM LINE

God's people have a great future with the perfect King.

→ TAKE IT FURTHER

More good news on page 124.

81 Figns and false prophets

**How can we know what to believe?
So many people say things that seem to
make sense, but how can we know if they
come from God?**

👁 Read Jeremiah 23 v 9–22

ENGAGE YOUR BRAIN

▶ What was wrong with these
guys who claimed to be God's
messengers? (v10, v13, v16–18)

▶ What marked out a true prophet
of God? (v22)

Signs that these men were not really
God's spokesmen included:
• using their power unfairly (v10)
• worshipping other gods (v13)
• not practising what they preached
• speaking their own minds, not
  God's words (v16)
• only giving good news (v17)
• not listening to God (v18)

It's not always easy to know if
someone really is teaching God's
truth. But these things above are all
warning signs. God's messengers
speak His words (from the Bible) and
turn people away from sinful ways
(v22). They don't just tell people what
they want to hear (v17).

👁 Read Jeremiah 24 v 1–10

▶ What promises did God make
to His faithful people? (v5–7)

▶ But what would happen to the
self-righteous people left in
Jerusalem? (v8–10)

No doubt the false prophets were
saying those left in Jerusalem were
safe and were favoured by God.
They were dead wrong and would
be punished severely for rejecting
God. But a great future lay ahead for
those who were sent into exile. And
God would deal with the root of the
problem — He would change their
hearts so they'd know and love Him!

PRAY ABOUT IT

This is true for God's people now
(Christians). God has changed their
hearts and brought them to know
Him. Will you thank Him for that?

→ TAKE IT FURTHER

Dreams and visions on page 124.

82 | Pain in the neck

Jeremiah preached God's words to the people of Judah. So did a guy called Hananiah. Or he claimed to. Which of them was right? If God's people chose wrongly, there would be serious consequences.

👁 **Read Jeremiah 27 v 1–11**

ENGAGE YOUR BRAIN

🔽 What was the point of Jeremiah's yoke around his neck? (v6–7)

🔽 What would everyone have to learn? (v5)

🔽 What was the big choice and the big consequences? (v8, v11)

🔽 What would making the right choice involve? (v12–15)

Jeremiah literally stuck his neck out for God. It must have been a hard message for the people to hear. But it was so important that Jeremiah took it to King Zedekiah (v12–15). And then he told God's people not to fall for false prophets who said God would soon reverse Nebuchadnezzar's plundering of Jerusalem (v16–22).

👁 **Read Jeremiah 28 v 1–17**

🔽 What did Hananiah claim God promised to do? (v2–4)

🔽 How did Jeremiah react? (v6–9)

🔽 What was the truth? (v13–14)

🔽 Why did God deal so severely with Hananiah? (v15–17)

Hananiah tried to water down Jeremiah's warnings. He was saying everything would be OK, don't worry about it. It's an easy thing to do, but we can't water down God's warnings and act as if they're no big deal.

GET ON WITH IT

🔽 How do you show that you trust God and what He's said?

PRAY ABOUT IT

Ask the Lord to help you take His warnings seriously and not listen to anyone who replaces God's words with positive-sounding lies.

➜ **TAKE IT FURTHER**

Missing chapters 25 and 26? They're covered on page 124.

83 | Dear figs...

King Nebuchadnezzar and the Babylonians were smashing all other nations. God used them to conquer Jerusalem and take some of God's people to live in Babylon. Jeremiah now writes to those exiles.

👁 Skim read chapter 29

ENGAGE YOUR BRAIN

▷ *Were they to expect God to take them home to Jerusalem soon? (v4–7)*

▷ *How long would they stay there? (v10)*

▷ *What would happen to those still in Jerusalem? (v15–16)*

▷ *Why? (v19)*

▷ *What would happen to the false prophets we've been reading about recently? (v20–23)*

👁 Read verses 10–14

▷ *What would happen after 70 years? (v10)*

▷ *What were God's plans for His people? (v11)*

▷ *What else did God promise His people? (v12–14)*

It's easy to think of Jeremiah as a prophet of gloom, but he was a messenger of true hope. He urged God's people to pin their hopes on God's great plans for them. Plans for prosperity, forgiveness and a return home. Despite their rebellion, God would listen to His people and give them great things (v11–12).

THINK IT OVER

Do you ever worry about an uncertain future? For Christians, the future is not uncertain. God promises to forgive His people, to take them home to live with Him and give them more than they could ever deserve.

PRAY ABOUT IT

Read verses 10–14 several times until you can't help but praise and thank our incredible God.

THE BOTTOM LINE

God has great plans for you.

→ TAKE IT FURTHER

Homework is on page 124.

84 | Big announcement

There has been loads of bad news for God's people in Jeremiah. It's been depressing reading at times. But not today. Brace yourself for some good news and the mind-blowing high point of the whole book.

👁 Read Jeremiah 30 v 1–11

ENGAGE YOUR BRAIN

▷ What's the good news for the exiles? (v3)

▷ What will the day of God's judgment be like for those who have rejected Him? (v5–7)

▷ What's the great news for God's people in the future? (v8–10)

▷ How should they look back on their time of exile? (v11)

👁 Read Jeremiah 31 v 31–40

▷ What's the big announcement? (v31–32)

▷ What is special about this new covenant agreement? (v33)

▷ What's the amazing news for God's people? (v34)

Read verses 31–34 again because this is incredible stuff. Jeremiah tells us of a new era for God's people. A time when God would write His law on our hearts. He wouldn't just tell His people how to live, but give them the desire and ability to live that way.

This time came with Jesus. His death launched the new covenant relationship with God. The cross signalled a new era in God dealing with His people. As we turn to Him, God forgives our sin and transforms our hearts. And there's no possibility of God reversing this promise (v36–37). Awesome.

PRAY ABOUT IT

This is news to sing and shout about! And to thank God for. Starting RIGHT NOW.

THE BOTTOM LINE
The future is bright for God's people.

→ TAKE IT FURTHER
Missing bits are located on page 124.

85 | Field of vision

I saw a brilliant magic trick in the countryside. A farmer turned his tractor into a field. OK, it's a terrible joke, but Jeremiah has got fields on his mind too.

👁 Read Jeremiah 32 v 1–9

ENGAGE YOUR BRAIN

- ▷ What was happening to Jerusalem? (v2)
- ▷ What was happening to Jeremiah? (v3)
- ▷ What surprising thing did God tell Jeremiah to do? (v8)

God had said Jerusalem would be conquered as punishment for their rebellion. This was now happening — the Babylonian army had surrounded Jerusalem and the city would soon fall. Meanwhile, Jeremiah had been locked up for giving King Zedekiah some straight talk. Seems a stupid time to buy a field!

👁 Read verses 16–25

- ▷ What's great about God? (v17–19)
- ▷ What had God done in the past? (v20–23)
- ▷ So why was Jeremiah confused? (v24–25)

Jeremiah knew God was powerful, miraculous and loving because of the great things He's done for His people. But now Jerusalem was under siege and suffering from famine and disease, and God asked Jeremiah to buy a field??? Had God lost His mind?

👁 Read verses 42–44
- ▷ What did God promise?

So, was it bizarre for Jeremiah to buy a field when the city's about to get trashed? No. It's God's way of illustrating how He would restore His people after His judgment. Brilliant.

PRAY ABOUT IT

Look back at the prayer in v17–23.

- ▷ What should God's action in the past remind us about?
- ▷ Which of the truths here will you remember as you pray?

→ TAKE IT FURTHER

Field some questions on page 124.

86 | Joy for Jerry in jail

Jeremiah's still locked up in prison and Jerusalem is still surrounded by the bloodthirsty Babylonians. All hope is lost, right? Wrong. God gives Jeremiah and all His people reasons to be cheerful.

👁 Read Jeremiah 33 v 1–13

ENGAGE YOUR BRAIN

▶ What's the not-so-surprising news? (v4–5)

▶ How would God turn things around? (v6–8)

▶ What would this lead to? (v9–11)

As we've heard before, it was too late for Jerusalem to escape God's punishment. But He promised to build a new, perfect Jerusalem. The great news is that because of Jesus, all believers will live in this wonderful community.

👁 Read verses 14–26

▶ What else did God promise? (v14–18)

▶ How does the New Testament show that God kept His promise?

David was king during Israel's golden years. But this great era didn't last

forever. Here God promises His people that out of David's family will come an even better king who would rule for ever. And this time the covenant relationship won't be broken. In fact, the sun would have to stop shining before God would abandon His people!

PRAY ABOUT IT

▶ How would you describe God's commitment to His people?

▶ How would you describe your commitment to God?

Use your answers to these to form the basis of your prayers now.

⟶ TAKE IT FURTHER

A tiny bit more on page 125.

87 Promise keepers

It's our last visit to Jeremiah for a while. Today it takes a bunch of outsiders to show God's people how to keep promises. It's a good reminder for us too.

👁 Read Jeremiah 34 v 8–22

ENGAGE YOUR BRAIN
- ▷ *What great thing did King Zed order? (v8)*
- ▷ *But what happened when the Babylonians stopped attacking Jerusalem? (v11)*
- ▷ *Why was this so bad? (v13–16)*
- ▷ *How did their actions backfire on them? (v17, v21–22)*

While the city was under siege, the upper classes were happy to free their slaves. After all, it meant fewer mouths to feed during the famine. But as soon as the Babylonians stopped attacking, they wanted their slaves back. Never mind that it meant breaking a covenant agreement with God. So God rightly handed them back into the hands of their slave-masters, the Babylonians.

👁 Read Jeremiah 35 v 1–19
- ▷ *Why did the Recabites not drink wine or build houses? (v8)*
- ▷ *What lesson could Judah learn from the Recabites? (v13–14)*
- ▷ *What made their actions even worse? (v15)*

The Recabites obeyed a human ancestor. But God's people in Judah wouldn't obey the Lord God Almighty! Despite His repeated warnings. They had completely earned their punishment.

GET ON WITH IT
- ▷ *Which of God's commands do you not stick to?*
- ▷ *How can you be a better example for Christian friends who struggle to live God's way?*

PRAY ABOUT IT
Pick two specific ways you need to be more obedient to your Father God. Now ask Him to help you be more willingly obedient to Him.

→ TAKE IT FURTHER
Great stuff on page 125. I promise.

88 | PSALMS: Head vs heart

Psalm 43 goes hand in hand with Psalm 42 (see day 63), as if they're one long song to God during difficult times.

👁 Read Psalm 43

ENGAGE YOUR BRAIN

▶ *What does this guy want from God? (v1)*

▶ *How does he feel about God? (v2)*

▶ *But what does he know God can do? (v3)*

▶ *What does he want to do when he's safe again? (v4)*

▶ *What conclusion does he come to? (v5)*

PAST

▶ *Can you think of any times you thought God had forgotten you?*

▶ *How did you respond?*

PRESENT

Think, using Psalms 42 and 43, how you should respond to God, whatever you're thinking or feeling.

▶ *Did the psalmist stop talking to God?*

▶ *Did he pretend to God that he was OK?*

▶ *How is he different at the end of 43 from the beginning of 42?*

FUTURE

▶ *Given today's example, how will you respond in future when you feel God's forgotten you?*

How we feel about God can be unreliable — all sorts of things upset us and make us feel God's forgotten us. It's in these times we need to remember who God is and what He's done. Both in history and in our lives. As Christians, we can remember what Jesus did on the cross. Let your head teach your heart how to respond.

PRAY ABOUT IT

Ask God to help you thirst for Him, longing to know Him better. Pray that what you know about Him will help you cope with how you feel.

→ TAKE IT FURTHER

No *Take it further* today. So read Psalms 42 and 43 again, noting down stuff that surprises you.

89 | I don't understand

Why is it that some of the nicest, most godly people seem to have the hardest lives? Suffering after suffering. It doesn't seem fair. Today's psalm writer had the same thing on his mind.

👁 Read Psalm 44 v 1–8

ENGAGE YOUR BRAIN

- ▶ What had God done for Israel in the past? (v2–3)

- ▶ What was He doing for them now? (v5–7)

- ▶ How did the people respond?

👁 Read verses 9–22

- ▶ But how did they feel about God now? (v9–16)

- ▶ What confused them? (v17–19)

If God wasn't punishing Israel for its sin, why was He letting them suffer? Why did it seem like He'd abandoned them?

👁 Read verses 23–26

- ▶ What did they accuse God of? (v23–24)

- ▶ What did they remember about God? (v26)

Still confused by bad stuff happening to good people? Take heart from the rest of the Bible. Unexplained suffering *will* make us wonder if God's gone. But it *actually* shows He's at work in us. It's because we belong to Him (*"for your sake"* v22). His great purpose is to make us like Jesus. That will mean suffering in this life. But what a privilege to suffer for Jesus, who died for us.

PRAY ABOUT IT

Tell God what's bothering and confusing you. Thank Him for His unfailing love. Ask Him to help you keep going when life is tough.

→ TAKE IT FURTHER

Brilliant news on page 125.

90 Wedding bells

You really need to smarten yourself up. Have a quick shower and then grab your poshest frock or smartest tie. After all, you've been invited to a royal wedding.

Read Psalm 45 v 1–9

ENGAGE YOUR BRAIN

▷ What's special about this royal bridegroom? (v2)

▷ Why is God impressed with him? (v7)

This is one special king. Not only is he hugely impressive and wealthy (v8), he speaks graciously (v2) and fights for truth, justice and righteousness (v4, v6). God approves of him and lifts him above other kings. No prizes for guessing who this king reminds us of. But what about his bride?

Read verses 10–17

▷ How will the bride and her bridesmaids look on the wedding day? (v13–15)

▷ Why won't it be difficult for her to be loyal to the king? (v11)

▷ Who will praise the king and for how long? (v17)

What a wedding. The rest of the Bible says these words about the groom (especially v6–7) are fulfilled in Jesus. Look again at v2–9 and 16–17. See how great He is?

What about the bride? Well, the New Testament tells us that the church (all believers) are Jesus' bride. One day the wedding will come and God's people will be fully united with Jesus, to live with the perfect King for ever. That's what I call a happy ending!

PRAY ABOUT IT

Use verses 2–7 to praise and thank God for His Son Jesus.

THE BOTTOM LINE

Jesus is the perfect King who will rule for ever.

→ TAKE IT FURTHER

Join the party on page 125.

91 | Safety instructions

Ever been anywhere you've felt in danger? And where do you feel safest? In this psalm, God's people find their security in God's city.

👁 **Read Psalm 46 v 1–3**

ENGAGE YOUR BRAIN

▷ *Is the psalm writer expecting huge or tiny trouble? (v2–3)*

▷ *So why isn't he cowering in his basement? (v1)*

It sounds as though the world is falling apart. Yet this guy knows God never leaves His people and always helps them through troubled times.

👁 **Read verses 4–7**

▷ *Why is God's city safe? (v5)*

▷ *What happens to God's enemies? (v6)*

Security is found in the city where God is present. Outside it is total disaster.

👁 **Read verses 8-11**

▷ *How would you describe God's power? (v8–9)*

▷ *How should we respond to this terrifying God? (v10)*

The Bible shows us over and over how immensely powerful the Lord is. Yet He wants us to know Him (v10) and have a close relationship with Him. Jesus has made this possible. And God protects His people, who will one day live with Him in His city.

PRAY ABOUT IT

Ask God to help you feel safe and secure as part of His family. Use the words of this psalm to help you praise Him.

→ **TAKE IT FURTHER**

Security code: P125.

107

TAKE IT FURTHER

If you want a little more at the end of each day's study, this is where you come. The TAKE IT FURTHER sections give you something extra. They look at some of the issues covered in the day's study, pose deeper questions, and point you to the big picture of the whole Bible.

EPHESIANS
Big big stuff

1 – SIMPLY THE BLESSED

Read verse 3 again
They are 'spiritual' blessings (so not a new phone etc), so we enjoy them in our relationship with Jesus through His Spirit. Count how often in v3–14 Paul says *'in him'* or *'in Christ'*.

Read verse 4
Before the creation, God put us and Jesus together in His mind. God determined to make us (who didn't yet exist) His children through the work of Christ (which hadn't yet taken place).

▶ *Did we deserve to be adopted into God's family?*
▶ *So how should we respond? (v6)*

2 – PERFECT PLAN

Read verse 14 again
Redemption is still to come. But haven't we got it already, according to v7? Well, both are true! God has brought us into His family. One day, that process will be complete when we're in God's presence.

▶ *Considering what God has done, how should we respond?*

3 – POWER-FILLED PRAYER

It's time to get specific in your prayers. List three Christians you get on well with and three you don't.

1.
2.
3.
4.
5.
6.

Spend two minutes praying for each of them. Thank God for them. Ask Him to help you show love to them. Pray that they will know God better, experience His power in their lives and live with Jesus ruling their lives.

4 – AMAZING GRACE

Re-read verses 1–10
▶ *What's true before we become Christians? (v1–3)*
▶ *What's true afterwards? (v4–10)*

Use these verses as a guide to help you explain how you became a Christian.

Write down your story, making sure it's a) honest, b) true to the Bible, c) makes Jesus central to the story.

5 – FREE PEACE, SWEET!

▶ *Since Jesus has destroyed the barrier between us and God (v16), and between us and other believers (v14), how should Christians behave?*

▶ *What walls of hostility do we build between each other?*

▶ *What part are you, yes you, playing in breaking these down?*

▶ *What can you do?*

▶ *How should v21–22 affect the way we treat each other?*

6 – OPEN SECRET

Read verse 8 again

Someone said: *'Paul combined personal humility with the authority of an apostle.'* You can see that great combination in v7–13. And when Paul talked about himself, he talked about Jesus.

▶ *Do you do that?*

▶ *Will you?*

▶ *How?*

7 – PAUL'S POWERFUL PRAYER

▶ *What can we learn from Paul's prayer?*

▶ *Which Christians can you pray for more regularly?*

▶ *What will you pray for them?*

▶ *How can you help others understand how great the love of Christ is?*

▶ *Any specific ideas?*

8 – ONE FAITH, ONE LORD

▶ *When are you most likely NOT to be humble or gentle or patient with other Christians?*

▶ *What steps are you going to take to change this?*

▶ *Why is it important you do? (v3)*

NUMBERS
Counting on God

9 – COUNT ME IN

The pattern we find in this part of the Bible, Redemption – Battle – Rest, is a good parallel of the Christian life. Like the Israelites, we have been rescued from slavery through Jesus' death in our place. We are heading for perfect rest in the new creation when Jesus returns. But we have a battle on our hands now as Satan is defeated but not destroyed and we live in a world hostile to God and His King, Jesus.

Read Ephesians 6 v 10–20 and use it as a basis for your prayers.

10 – GIFTS TO GOD

Have you ever heard or sung the hymn *'Take My Life'*? Read the words now and use it as a basis for your prayers.

Take my life and let it be
Consecrated, Lord, to Thee;
Take my hands and let them move
At the impulse of Thy love.

Take my feet and let them be
Swift and beautiful for Thee;
Take my voice and let me sing,
Always, only for my King.

Take my lips and let them be
Filled with messages from Thee;
Take my silver and my gold,
Not a mite would I withhold.

Take my moments and my days,
Let them flow in endless praise;
Take my intellect and use
Every power as Thou shalt choose.

Take my will and make it Thine,
It shall be no longer mine;
Take my heart, it is Thine own,
It shall be Thy royal throne.

Take my love, my Lord, I pour
At Thy feet its treasure store;
Take myself and I will be
Ever, only, all for Thee.

11 – MOVING ON
Read Hebrews 10 v 1–4
and v11–18
▷ *What were the limitations of the Old*
   Testament sacrificial system?
▷ *Why is Jesus' death better?*
▷ *What new blessing do Christians have*
   which Israel didn't? (v16)

12 – MOANING MIRIAM
Do you ever moan about your leaders at
church or youth group? Be aware of the
damage it can cause. If you have an issue,
discuss it directly with the person involved;
don't grumble to everyone else.

See what Jesus has to say when his
disciple act like Miriam and Aaron:
Mark 9 v 33–35 and
Mark 10 v 35–45.

13 – YOUR NUMBER'S UP
The big issue in chapters 13–14 wasn't the
size of the opposition. Or the number of
people in the land. Or the Israelites' own
ability. It was this:
▷ *Would God's people trust His promise*
   and act on it?
▷ *Or would they retreat in fear and lack*
   of faith?

The story of God's people failing to go on
trusting God crops up, sadly, too often in
the Bible.
Read Hebrews 3 v 7–14
▷ *What lesson do v12–14 urge you*
   to learn?

14 – PROMISES, OFFERINGS AND TASSELS
Read verses 30–36
Is God's reaction (v35–36) over the top?
No. God had given the Sabbath to God's
people for them to rest. A failure to keep
it was going against God. How could such
a person remain in God's presence after
defying Him like that?

15 – CARRY ON GRUMBLING
Spend some time thinking about what it
means for Jesus to be our perfect High
Priest. **Hebrews 4 v 14 – 5 v 5, 7 v 23–27**

and 9 v 24 – 10 v 14 are good places to start.

16 – BUDDING CAREER

In the Old Testament, we get plenty of reminders that God is holy — see **Exodus 3 v 5–6** and **Isaiah 6 v 1–5** for starters. But remind yourself of Peter's early encounter with Jesus in **Luke 5 v 1–11** and think about why Peter responded as he did.

17 – GIVE IT BACK
Read Numbers 19 v 1–22
▶ *What makes people 'unclean'?*
▶ *What does God's solution involve? (v1-8)*

When sinful people come into contact with a holy God, death is the only outcome. So how are the people to be cleansed and purified? By blood — an animal's death in their place.

Read Hebrews 9 v 13–14
▶ *What replaced the death of an animal to purify people?*
▶ *So how should we respond?*

EPHESIANS 4–6

18 – BIG BIG STUFF
▶ *Why is it good that God's church is made up of different sorts of people?*
▶ *What will it be like to be involved in it?*
▶ *What 'works of service' could you do for people in your church?*

▶ *What needs can you help with?*
▶ *So... when will you do it?*

19 – SPOT THE DIFFERENCE
Read verses 17–19 and then Romans 1 v 18–32
Notice the same process in those who reject God's rule over them — a *hard heart* leads to a *dead mind* leads to a *dead soul* leads to *reckless living*. That's all a mark of God's punishment.

Spot the difference between Ephesians 4 v 17–19 and 20–24. Don't let anyone kid you there's no real difference between a Christian and a non-Christian. So live out that difference, don't hide it!

20 – DOS AND DON'TS
Read verses 25–32 again. Slowly.
▶ *Is there any one verse here that stands out for you?*
▶ *Why does it stand out?*
▶ *Will your lifestyle reflect that you're one of God's new people?*
▶ *How will you make that happen?*

21 – GREAT IMPRESSIONS
Read verses 5–6
This is not talking about a Christian who falls back into sin sometimes. It's about those who have given themselves over to living this way.
▶ *How might we be deceived into thinking that this sort of behaviour doesn't really matter?*

22 – WASTE OF TIME?

For more on alcohol, try these:

Proverbs 20 v 1
Proverbs 23 v 31–35
1 Corinthians 6 v 19–20

▷ *How does your attitude towards drinking need to change?*
▷ *So what will you do?*

If you're tempted by heavy drinking, talk to another Christian about it, so they can pray for you and check up on you.

23 – MARRIAGE = CHURCH?

Men and women are equal before God, but have different roles.

▷ *Why is this biblical principle exciting?*

If you're single but think you might get married one day...

▷ *Are you prepared to live as v22–33 command?*
▷ *How would some of your attitudes have to change?*
▷ *How does Paul summarise his teaching on marriage? (v33)*

24 – HOME, WORK

Read verse 1 again

'*In the Lord*' means recognising God's authority in all this, and the roles He intends for parents and children.

▷ *Do you communicate in a way that shows respect to them?*

Read Colossians 3 v 17

▷ *What would happen if you actually obeyed this command?*

▷ *So... what will you do about it?*

25 – ARMOUR OF GOD

Read verses 11–14,
James 4 v 7
and 1 Peter 5 v 8–9

All we have to do against the devil is to stand. Don't go looking for him to pick a fight. Simply be 'strong in the Lord' and what He's done for us. And stand. With God, you can do that, even when it seems impossible.

▷ *How can we help each other to be 'strong in the Lord'?*
▷ *What might be some of the devil's schemes against us?*
▷ *What poses the greatest threat to your faith?*

26 – PRAY HARD

Well done, you've read all of Ephesians! Paul's letter has shown God's new order and His new orders. Thank God for making you part of His people and plan.

▷ *What have you learned from Ephesians?*
▷ *How can you live differently for God?*

NUMBERS 20-36

27 – COUNTING ON GOD

Chapter 20 may be a catalogue of disappointments but what do we find out that we need?

• A perfectly obedient leader (v12)
• An all powerful king (v20–21)

• A High Priest who lives forever (v28–29) Can you think of some New Testament passages which show that Jesus meets all these requirements? See if you can find some...

28 – SNAKES ALIVE!

▷ What does Jesus say about the bronze serpent? (John 3 v 14–15)

▷ What problem did the bronze serpent deal with?

▷ What problem does the cross deal with?

▷ What did the Israelites have to do to be saved?

▷ What about us?

29 – PROPHET PROFIT

For more on Balaam, check out Deuteronomy 23 v 4–5, 2 Peter 2 v 15–16, Jude 11 and Revelation 2 v 14

▷ What do we learn about his character and actions?

30 – DON'T BE A DONKEY

When God's enemies try their hardest to curse God's people, it often backfires. The early church in Jerusalem was persecuted but the gospel message still spread to Judea and Samaria (Acts 8 v 1). As some guy called Tertullian put it: *"The blood of the martyrs is the seed of the church".* Even today, atheist books and advertising campaigns result in more people examining the claims of Christianity for themselves. Thank God for His incredible control over history.

31 – THE DESTROYER

Check out one of the most famous prophesies about Israel's king — Deuteronomy 17 v 14–20.

▷ How did David and Solomon measure up? (1 Kings 10 v 23 – 11 v 13)

▷ How about Jesus?

32 – SEDUCTION TECHNIQUE

Look again at verses 4–5

▷ Do you take sin as seriously as God does?

▷ Why/why not?

▷ How does the cross show how seriously God takes sin and how much He loves us?

33 – TIME FOR A RECOUNT

Read 1 Corinthians 10 v 1–13

▷ What lessons have you learned from Numbers?

Write them down somewhere where you will be reminded of them.

34 – HERE COME THE GIRLS

As God's people today, we're not looking forward to being in a particular place. God's promise to us is bigger and smaller than that. Firstly, it's smaller because we find our rest "in Christ" not "in the land". But secondly, it's bigger because when Jesus returns, His people will inherit the whole earth (Matthew 5 v 5)!

35 – OUT FOR THE COUNT

Go back and look at chapters 28–30 if you didn't get a chance to do it all earlier.

▷ *What do these verses remind us of?*
  28 v 15, v22, v30,
  29 v 5, v11, v16, v19, v22, v25,
  29 v 28, v31, v34, v38

▷ *What impact would this have had on the people as these festivals cropped up throughout the year?*

▷ *How are things different for God's people after Jesus' death and resurrection?*

36 – LAST ORDERS

Read Numbers 31 v 19–54

These verses explain the aftermath of the war: how the soldiers were to be made fit to be in God's presence again and how all the loot was to be shared out fairly.

▷ *What would this plunder keep reminding the people of? (v54)*

37 – NUMBERING OFF

Check out Numbers 33 v 55-56 again

▷ *Do you think the Israelites heeded that warning?*

Read Psalm 106 — it sums up how Israel would behave from the Exodus to the Exile.

▷ *What was Israel's problem time and again?*

▷ *What hope do v44–48 offer?*

▷ *What hope does Jesus offer?*

LUKE
Walking with Jesus

38 – DON'T DON'T DON'T

Read verse 10 again

Some people worry they've committed the unforgivable sin. Listen up. Verses like John 3 v 16 and 3 v 36 say everyone who trusts in Jesus will be forgiven and saved. Eternal life hangs on knowing or rejecting Jesus.

So... blasphemy against the Spirit must be the same as rejecting Jesus. It's the Holy Spirit's job to make Jesus known to people. If someone refuses to have anything to do with Jesus, they are refusing the Spirit's work and rejecting Jesus. **Check out Romans 8 v 9–11.**

39 – FAT CAT FATE

Read verse 15

One of the best ways to relax your grip on possessions is to be happy to lend them out. Are you prepared to take that risk?

Read verse 21

Is Jesus saying we shouldn't save money? No. He's saying: *Don't think life is just about how much you've got in the bank.* It may be wise to save money. But don't start thinking the money is yours. It's not. God gave it to you on loan. The same goes for your possessions.

▷ *How much money do you get a week?*

▷ *Read v21 again. What are you using it for?*

40 – DON'T WORRY, BE HAPPY
Read Philippians 4 v 4–7

▶ *What are we to do? (v4)*

▶ *What are we not to do? (v6a)*

▶ *What else are we to do? (v6)*

When you feel anxious, turn that anxiety into a prayer to God. Give the worry to God, because He's in control and is near — and then stop worrying about it as if you're the one in control!

Read Luke 12 v 31

Seeking His kingdom means obeying Him in our lives and urging others to recognise that God is in control and should rule their lives.

▶ *How will you make this your priority?*

41 – GET READY
For more on Jesus returning, **read 2 Peter 3 v 8–13.**

▶ *Jesus will return in person. How does that change the way...*
a) you talk to Him?
b) you live now?
c) you talk to your friends?

▶ *How are you using your God-given abilities and opportunities?*

42 – OUR PLACE IN HISTORY
It's not easy living in a family divided because some are Christians and some aren't. If you're still living at home, there's a very encouraging and challenging verse in Colossians: *"Children, obey your parents in everything, for this pleases the Lord."* (Colossians 3 v 20)

Encouragement — by obeying your parents, even when you disagree with their decision, you can please Jesus. Being a Christian teenager doesn't exempt you from obeying your folks — in fact it makes it even more important! And as you grow in obedience, it's a great example to your parents if they're not Christians.

Challenge — It's not easy to obey! And it's very unfashionable to obey! So pray that God will help you do it!

43 – DISASTER STRIKES
Why does God let disasters happen? Where is God in a world of suffering? Here's what the Bible says on the subject.

1. Jesus showed God's huge care for our world by undergoing the greatest suffering of all — separated and punished by God — on the cross.
2. Just like in today's Luke bit, disasters are reminders of how much worse being on the wrong side of God's final judgment will be.
3. For the Christian, suffering makes us more like Jesus. **See 1 Peter 4 v 12–19 and Romans 8 v 28–39.**

Are sinful people punished with suffering? There are some cases in the Bible where God acts in that way. But He has delayed His total, final punishment until Jesus comes back. **Check out 2 Thessalonians 1 v 6–10 and 2 Peter 3 v 9.**

44 – JESUS VS RELIGION
Read Luke 13 v 18–21

▶ What's Jesus talking about? (v18)

▶ How big does a mustard seed start?

▶ What does it go on to become? (v19)

▶ What happened to the yeast in the dough? (v20–21)

▶ As Jesus spoke, the kingdom of God on earth numbered a few dozen people — what would happen to it?

▶ What should we expect to see happening to the kingdom of God in our day?

45 – BEST PARTY EVER

The Bible is clear that our own efforts, or *works*, don't save us (Ephesians 2 v 8–9). Trusting in Jesus is the way to God's kingdom (John 14 v 6). The "effort" that Jesus is talking about in Luke 13 v 24 is not making an effort to be saved, but making an effort to keep following the one who has saved us.

46 – FOX AND HENS

The Jews were meant to be God's people. But the Old Testament is full of examples of them ignoring God's prophets, because they didn't like what they said. Jeremiah was God's messenger, but was opposed consistently throughout his life. You can read of one such episode of opposition in Jeremiah 37 v 1 – 38 v 13.

In Luke 13 v 33–34, Jesus clearly knows, based on Jerusalem's past record with prophets like Jeremiah, what He as God's own Son should expect to face — death.

47 – FOOD FOR THOUGHT
Read verses 12–14

Tricky stuff. Jesus isn't saying: When you have a party, invite only people you don't like (although that might be good for us). It probably means we should value those who are in God's kingdom, whatever they are like. And we're not to do it looking for a reward in this life (v14).

▶ Embarrassed by some of your Christian/church friends?

▶ Who do you need to change your attitude towards?

48 – RSVP

In 13 v 24, Jesus underlined that entering the narrow door, following him to eternal life, requires our effort. But in 14 v 23, we're reminded that being saved is also God's initiative; He sent Jesus to "make them come in, so that my house will be full." Both 13 v 24 and 14 v 23 are true; we need to decide to turn to Jesus and follow him to have eternal life, but we're only able to do that because God sent Jesus to show us who He is and what He offers — to pick us up and carry us through that narrow door into God's kingdom.

JEREMIAH
Prophet in pain

49 – A CALL FOR JEREMIAH
Read verse 5 again

A reminder of how very intimately God knows us.

▶ *How should this make us respond to Him?*

Read verses 11–12

The almond branch thing seems weird and confusing. The language Jeremiah spoke was Hebrew. In Hebrew, the world for "almond tree" *(saqed)* is similar to the verb "watch" *(saqad)*. The point was that God was watching and making sure His words came true (v12). Whatever He tells Jeremiah to say will actually happen.

50 – COURT IN THE ACT
Read verses 14–19

God's people brought God's punishment on themselves. They had broken their covenant agreement with God. As a result, they were invaded (v15) and ruled by the Egyptians (v16). So why slope back to those enemies for comfort? (v18)

▶ *What warning does v19 give us?*

51 – RETURN TICKET
Jeremiah 3 v 1 is a summary of **Deuteronomy 24 v 1–4**. The chapter works like this: Could a woman who's got married then divorced, married again and divorced, return to her first husband? (v3a) Under Old Testament law the answer was

no. So could Israel, who had abandoned God's covenant and taken up with false gods, return to God as before? (v3b) Under the principle of Old Testament law the answer is still no. But in God's grace the answer is yes! He would let His adulterous people return to Him (3 v 12, 14–18; 4 v 2).

Read Jeremiah 3 v 16

They will no longer say *"the ark of the covenant"* — what's all that about? The ark (a box which symbolised God's presence and rule among His people) would one day not be needed. But why not? Because God would live among His people again, through His Spirit (that's happening now). And ultimately in the new heavens and new earth. (More about that in **Revelation 21 and 22**.)

52 – POETIC JUSTICE

God's judgment sounds harsh. But is it? Think what follows if God can't be be bothered to judge.

▶ *What would it say about His attitude to our sin?*

▶ *What would that mean for the way we run our lives?*

▶ *What sort of God would that make Him?*

Read verse 10

As part of His judgment, God let Judah's prophets tell the people: Everything's fine. We'll be OK.

Speaking of God's judgment made

Jeremiah sick to his stomach, but he did so because he desperately cared about his people.

- ▷ *Do you feel so strongly, knowing some of your friends and family are facing God's punishment?*
- ▷ *What will you do about it?*

53 – JUST ONE GOOD MAN!
Read Jeremiah 6 v 1–15
Tekoa and Beth Hakkeram (v1) were places to run away to south of Jerusalem.

- ▷ *Had God's people shown any sign of change? (v7)*
- ▷ *What does v8 remind us about God?*

Even at this late stage, there's a chance. God orders Judah's destruction (v6), but wants them to turn to Him (v8).

The people were so hard-hearted they were incapable of change (v10–13). They'd buried the ability to feel any twinge of guilt.

- ▷ *Know anyone like that?*

Don't give up on them; it might not be too late. Keep asking God to rescue them.

54 – DON'T READ THIS PAGE
Read Jeremiah 7 v 21–34
God's saying: You eat your stupid offerings. What's the point of them when you refuse to obey me, despite all I offer?

- ▷ *How had they got things badly wrong? (v22–26)*
- ▷ *What would this nation be remembered for? (v27–29)*

God's people burned babies. And claimed

it was God's idea!!! No chance (v31).

- ▷ *What would happen to these killers? (v32–34)*

55 – IDOL TALK
Read Jeremiah 8 v 18 – 9 v 11
Jeremiah and God, in turn, express grief and exasperation that God's people remain blind to what's going on, refusing to turn to Him.

Jesus also wept for Jerusalem.
Read Luke 19 v 41–44

- ▷ *What breaks God's heart?*
- ▷ *How does this remind us to pray for non-Christian friends?*

56 – SLAUGHTER THEM, GOD!
Read Jeremiah 11 v 1–17

- ▷ *Was God's coming judgment unfair? (v3–4, v7–8)*

God's people would get what they deserved. The big shock was that God delayed that punishment for so long. But the failure of God's people would come back to haunt them (v11–15). Verse 15 is saying: How on earth could God's people be so two-faced and hypocritical?

- ▷ *What's the warning for us?*

57 – BELT UP!
Read Jeremiah 13 v 18–27

- ▷ *What's the message to the king and queen mother of Judah? (v18–20)*
- ▷ *What should we expect if we hang out with God's enemies? (v21)*
- ▷ *What happens if you make a habit of rebelling against God? (v23–24)*

58 – GOD'S DEADLINE
Read Jeremiah 14 v 13 – 15 v 9
▷ *What do we learn about Jeremiah's character?*
▷ *And his job?*
▷ *And his relationship with God?*
▷ *What do you have in common with Jeremiah?*
▷ *How are you different from him?*
▷ *How's your relationship with God right now?*

59 – WHO DO YOU TRUST?
Read Jeremiah 16 v 1–21
▷ *What was Jeremiah banned from? (v2, v5, v8)*
▷ *Why?*

Jeremiah's painfully isolated life would show God's people how unbearable life would be under His judgment. God was so concerned to get His message across that He made Jeremiah's *life* teach it! Jeremiah was told not to marry at all, which was totally unheard of back then. It showed that the relationship between God and His people was now over.

Read Jeremiah 17 v 13–27
and jot down what you learn about
a) Judah
b) Jeremiah
c) God
d) yourself.
More from Jeremiah in a few weeks...

PSALMS

60 – STEWING IN SILENCE
Read verses 4–8 again
▷ *What truths did David recognise about life and God? (v5–6)*
▷ *When thinking about death, what was David's reaction? (v7)*
▷ *What was his plea? (v8)*
▷ *Why do you think he prayed this?*

He'd seen how vital it is, in the face of death, to know God's forgiveness. And he asked for God's mercy (v10, v13) before his life ends.
▷ *What reminders has this psalm brought home to you?*
▷ *What has it raised that you need to talk to God about?*
▷ *Unlike David, we live after Jesus' death and resurrection. How must this change our outlook on life and death?*

61 – MOOD MUSIC
Read verses 6–8, then read Hebrews 10 v 1–10
▷ *What was the purpose of Old Testament sacrifices? (v3)*
▷ *What couldn't they do? (v4)*
▷ *How has Jesus replaced Old Testament sacrifices? (v10)*

62 – HIGHS AND LOWS
Does verse 9 sound familiar? Jesus used it to speak of His own experience.
Find it in John 13 v 18–30

63 – HEART ACHE

For Old Testament Israelites, God's presence was in the temple. So, to worship Him, you went there and offered a sacrifice to Him. But today we don't have a temple where God is specially present. So how do we get to God and worship Him?

**Read Hebrews 10 v 11–14
and Hebrews 13 v 11–16**

▶ *How were the sacrifices the high priest made a picture of what Jesus did?*

▶ *In what ways was Jesus' sacrifice far better?*

▶ *How do we now worship God? (Hebrews 13 v 5–6)*

LUKE 14–18

64 – WALKING WITH JESUS

Read verses 33–35

▶ *What will being a disciple mean for us and our possessions?*

Is Jesus saying we should throw it all away? Read it again. It's more than being ready to give things up; it's actually doing it. That's when it's real. Salt's only good if it is actually salty. A disciple is only a real one if he/she will give up anything to follow Jesus. What's in view is life for ever with God Himself. What makes that possible for us is the death of Jesus. So we must be quick to give up everything to put Him first — relationships (v26), what we own (v33), even our lives (v27). Nothing can mean more to us than Jesus.

65 – GET READY TO PARTY

In Luke 15 v 7, Jesus talks about *"ninety-nine righteous persons who do not need to repent"*. But elsewhere, the Bible says: *"There is no one righteous, not even one"* (Romans 3 v 10). Jesus isn't telling the Pharisees they're already righteous (right with God); His big point is that His priority is to find those who are outside God's kingdom and bring them in. As He'll explain in His next parable, both those who ignore God and those who think they're good enough are outside God's kingdom. No one is righteous — Pharisees included.

67 – THANKS, DAD!

In Jesus' parable, the father was willing to leave his house and humiliate himself in public in order to welcome his son — and that's a picture of what God's done to welcome us into His kingdom.

Check out Luke 22 v 63 – 23 v 46
and, as you read, think: God the Son left heaven and did all this so He could welcome me into His home. Then talk to God.

68 – MONEY MONEY MONEY

Read verses 16–18

The teaching of the Old Testament (*"the Law and the Prophets"*) had now been followed by new teaching (v16). Jesus had arrived and people could receive eternal life by trusting in His rescue. But that doesn't mean the Old Testament is no longer important. It is still essential reading — it points to Jesus! In v18, Jesus mentioned one way He fully respected the Old Testament.

In v18, Jesus briefly mentions marriage and divorce. In our society (as in those days), it's very easy to get divorced. But marriage is God's invention (Genesis 2 v 21–25), and He invented it to be lifelong. So Jesus is here making clear that divorce and remarriage should not be taken lightly; in fact, people who get divorced primarily so they can get together with someone else are committing adultery. Marriage is great; marriage is for life; take it seriously!

69 – A SERIOUS WARNING

Is this parable saying the rich go to hell and the poor go to heaven? No. The point here is the need to make up your mind in this life about Jesus.

▶ How do the two stories in chapter 16 make the same point?

Read verse 31 again
Ever heard someone say: "If God proved to me He was real, I'd believe."?

▶ How would you answer them?
▶ According to v31, is any more evidence needed?

70 – YOUR PROBLEM, MY PROBLEM
Look up Ephesians 4 v 25–32
Verse 32 is very helpful — it reminds us that knowing how we should treat others is really simple — we're to treat others as God treats us. It's always so easy to hold

a grudge and not forgive someone when they let us down or upset us. But if we remember that through Jesus God has forgiven us all the times we've ignored, disobeyed and disappointed Him, then suddenly forgiving a friend won't seem like such a big deal anymore.

71 – WHO'S ON WHOSE SIDE?
Read Acts 3 v 1–26
This is a great example of how powerfully God works through His people. Peter heals this man "in the name of Jesus Christ". It's Christ's power, not Peter's faith, that matters. And so when the onlookers stare at Peter as though he's amazingly powerful (v12), Peter points them not to himself but to God's Son, Jesus — because it's having faith in Him that counts (v16). It's not about the size of Peter's faith; it's about the power of Jesus working through His faithful servant, Peter.

72 – THANKS, GOD
The healing was a living illustration of the Pharisees' response to Jesus' teaching. And a challenge.
▶ How will you be like the one man?
▶ Brainstorm everything you want to thank God for, and everything there is to praise Him about.
▶ How will you show heart-felt thanks to God in the way you do things over the next few days?

73 – JESUS: THE RETURN

Read verse 32
and then Genesis 19 v 1–26

God had decided to destroy Sodom and Gomorrah, two massively sinful cities; but He'd also decided to rescue a man named Lot and his family, since Lot was a godly man. The Lord sent angels to tell Lot's family to get out of the city (v12–17). Lot and his family ran to a town called Zoar (v22) and were spared. God had rescued them — but Lot's wife looked back, regretting the life she'd left behind — and was turned into a pillar of salt (v26).

Jesus' point is this — when He returns, we're not to be like her, looking back to our old lives and regretting leaving them behind. When Jesus returns, we should be so thankful that He's rescued us and so excited about eternity with Him that we never want to look back.

74 – DO SOMETHING, GOD!

If God will bring perfect justice to His persecuted people when Jesus returns, why doesn't Jesus return now? Why didn't He return centuries ago? In his second letter, Jesus' disciple Peter tells us...

Check out 2 Peter 3 v 8–10

"The day of the Lord will come" (v10) — and God isn't slow in keeping His promise to judge the world (v9). Why hasn't He come back yet? Because He's being patient (v9), giving people (perhaps you!) time to repent, so that when He returns they won't perish but will have eternal life. So, if we're Christians, we're to spend this time before Jesus returns praying that He would bring justice, but also telling people how they can enjoy life with Jesus instead of facing judgment on "the day of the Lord".

75 – COMPARE AND CONTRAST

Read verses 15–17

The disciples try to stop children getting to Jesus (v15).

▷ *But Jesus tells them not to stop the children — because who does the kingdom of God belong to? (end of v16)*

▷ *What does He add in v17?*

Read verses 13–14

▷ *Tricky question — How does what Jesus says in v15–17 reinforce His parable in v 9–14?*

That tax collector was like a child. He came to God not offering Him anything, or thinking he deserved anything, but simply asking Him for mercy.

76 – ALL YOU NEED

Look up Philippians 3 v 4–9

In v4–6, Paul lists loads of reasons for him having "confidence in the flesh" (relying on who he is and what he does to get eternal life).

▷ *What does he now think of those things compared to knowing and following Jesus? (v7–8)*

▷ *What has he realised is the only way to have "righteousness" (being right with God)? (end of v9)*

Paul had realised what the rich ruler missed — having eternal life is not about what you do: it's about who you know. It's not about being good, but about trusting in Jesus' death on the cross.

77 – BLIND FAITH

Jesus describes Himself as the *"Son of Man"* (v31); the blind beggar calls Him *"Son of David"*. Both are hugely significant names…

Read Daniel 7 v 13–14
▷ *What do we find out about the son of man?*

Check out 2 Samuel 7 v 12–16
Here God is speaking to King David.
▷ *What does God promise David about one of his descendants?*

JEREMIAH 19–35

78 – PROPHET IN PAIN

Other Bible bits that describe God as a potter: **Genesis 2 v 7–8, v19**
Psalm 95 v 5
Romans 9 v 19–21

Did you spot the difference between the pot pictures in chapters 18 and 19? In chapter 18, Judah was still given an opportunity to be changed by the potter's hand. In chapter 19, it's too late. A pot smashed to smithereens signifies irreversible destruction.

79 – STOCKS AND SHARES

Read Jeremiah 21 v 1–10
Remember how they'd treated Jeremiah before? (20 v 1–2).
▷ *Now, when emergency struck, what did Zedekiah and his cronies do?*
▷ *But what's their motive? (v2)*
▷ *What would they have to learn? (v3–7)*

It's all too late. Judgment is coming. It's death or exile (v8–9).

Now grab God's other verdicts. Take at least 3 from the list below. Read them and use the questions (below) with each one.
21 v 11–14: God vs an unnamed king
22 v 1–5: and another
22 v 6–10: and another one too
22 v 11–12: God vs Shallum
22 v 13–19: God vs Jehoiakim
22 v 20–23 God vs Jerusalem the city
22 v 24–30: God vs Jehoiachin

▷ *What was God's message?*
▷ *And the reason for it?*
▷ *What truths does it force you to remember?*

80 – BACK TO THE FUTURE

**Read verse 6 again,
then Romans 3 v 21–26**
▷ *What's the good news in these verses?*
▷ *What does the cross tell us about God?*
▷ *What has happened to God's anger? (v25)*
▷ *How does the cross show God's*

justice? (v26)

▣ And God's love?

81 – FIGS AND FALSE PROPHETS
Read Jeremiah 23 v 23–32

▣ What must we remember about God? (v23–24)

▣ Where were these guys going wrong? (v25–27)

▣ What should they have known? (v28–29)

▣ What would they learn? (v30–32)

God did speak through dreams in the Old Testament (Genesis 28, Daniel 2). But it seems these prophets were claiming any dream was the word of God and interpreting it any way they wanted to.

Read verses 33–40

Oracle = announcement. The prophets and people might forget God, but they'd never forget His coming judgment (v39–40).

82 – PAIN IN THE NECK
Read Jeremiah 25 v 1–11

▣ What was God's first challenge to His people? (v3)

▣ What had been their constant response? (v4–7)

▣ Why was the action of God's people so stupid? (v5)

▣ But who was in control, and what would He do? (v9–11)

Read Jeremiah 26 v 1–24

▣ What was God's repeated message to His people? (v3–6)

▣ How did the people respond to Jeremiah's message? (v8–11)

▣ What was the court's verdict? (v16)

▣ What did they remember? (v17–19)

83 – DEAR FIGS...

Your homework today is short but vital: **learn Jeremiah 29 v 11**.

84 – BIG ANNOUNCEMENT
Read Jeremiah 30 v 12–24

▣ What would God do for His people? (v18–20)

▣ What must they remember? (v23–24)

Read Jeremiah 31 v 1–30

▣ How does God show His love? (v3–6)

▣ What will life be like for God's people? (v8–14)

▣ How would the people respond to their punishment? (v18–19)

▣ What else does God promise? (v23–25)

85 – FIELD OF VISION

Jeremiah buying a field is doubly good. It's not just showing that God would restore His people, but it's God restoring Jeremiah to his family too. He had been cut off from mixing with his own people. Now all would change: Jeremiah was living out Israel's future. Clever, huh?

Read verses 26–41

Here God gives a reminder of His loyalty to His rebellious people. Verse 27 (and verse 17) is quoting God's words from Genesis 18 v 14.

⚪ When do you need to remember this?

⚪ What bad habits. situations, difficulties or people have you given up on that you need now to bring back to God?

86 – JOY FOR JERRY IN JAIL
Read verse 3 again

God hasn't promised to reveal new truth to us. But when we ask Him, God does enable us to understand the truths that He's already revealed to us in the Bible.

⚪ Do you take Him up on that offer?

87 – PROMISE KEEPERS
Read Jeremiah 34 v 1–7

Why was it right that the city got burned? Well, God's punishment always fits the crime. **Check out Jeremiah 7 v 31, 19 v 5, 36 v 32.**

Read John 14 v 23–24 and John 15 v 14–15

⚪ What does it mean to obey God?

⚪ What will it mean for YOU to obey God?

⚪ How's it going at the moment?

89 – I DON'T UNDERSTAND!
Read verse 22 and Romans 8 v 35–39

These verses in Romans are so reassuring! Whoever may be against us, God is greater, and He won't abandon us or let us go. Because He loves us. Whatever the opposition, danger or difficulties that tempt us to give up, nothing will separate us from Jesus' love, or from sharing His victory (v37).

⚪ What things are you most afraid of? Add them to Paul's list in v38–39. And thank God that not even those things can stop His plans or His love for you.

90 – WEDDING BELLS
Read Revelation 19 v 6–9

⚪ When Jesus returns, why will God's people celebrate?

⚪ What will the party be like?

If you're a Christian, you'll be part of this amazing wedding celebration. So join in the shout from verses 6 and 9!

91 – SAFETY INSTRUCTIONS

⚪ How difficult is it for you to remember that God is an ever-present help in trouble? What would help that?

Read Revelation 21 v 1–5

⚪ What will happen to the earth as we know it?

⚪ Where will God be in this new earth?

⚪ God is with His people now by His Spirit, but how will the eternal city be mind-blowingly better? (v3–4)

engage wants to hear from YOU!

▶ Share experiences of God at work in your life
▶ Any questions you have about the Bible or the Christian life?
▶ How can we make *engage* even better?

Email us — **martin@thegoodbook.co.uk**

(Unlike in previous issues, this email address actually works!)

Or use the space below to write us a quick note. You can post it to:

engage 37 Elm Road, New Malden, Surrey, KT3 3HB, UK

In the next engage

Philippians Pure joy
Deuteronomy Devoted to God
Luke Last days of Jesus
Jeremiah God's judgment
Plus: What's so bad about sin?
    How do I become a
    Christian?
    Big Bible words
    War

Order engage now!

Make sure you order the next issue of engage. Or even better, grab a one-year subscription to make sure engage lands in your hands as soon as it's out.

Call us to order in the UK on **0845 225 0880**
International: **+44 (0) 20 8942 0880**

or visit your friendly neighbourhood website:
UK: www.thegoodbook.co.uk
N America: www.thegoodbook.com
Australia: www.thegoodbook.com.au
New Zealand: www.thegoodbook.co.nz

DON'T PANIC!

The Ultimate Exam Survival Kit

Exams are a time of real stress for many young Christians – their future resting on their results. It's a time when they most need the guidance and reassurance that God's word can give to them. That's why we've developed **Don't Panic** - a new exam survival guide.

It includes 20 daily Bible readings for stressed-out students, revision timetables, and practical short articles on doing revision, exam technique and dealing with stress. Get hold of a copy of **Don't Panic** for yourself, or for school or college students you know who will be facing exams this summer.